Skyhorse Publishing books may be purchased in bulk at special discounts for sales
promotion, corporate gifts, fund-raising, or educational purposes. Special editions can
also be created to specifications. For details, contact the Special Sales Department,
Skyhorse Publishing, 307 West 36th Street, 11th Floor, New York, NY 10018 or
info@skyhorsepublishing.com.

Skyhorse® and Skyhorse Publishing® are registered trademarks of
Skyhorse Publishing, Inc.®, a Delaware corporation.

Visit our website at www.skyhorsepublishing.com.

10 9 8 7 6 5 4 3 2 1

Library of Congress Cataloging-in-Publication Data is available on file.

Cover design by David Ter-Avanesyan
Cover images by Lena Granefelt

Print ISBN: 978-1-5107-6904-5
Ebook ISBN: 978-1-5107-7047-8

Printed in China

NO-DIG GARDENING

RAISED BEDS, LAYERED GARDENS, AND OTHER NO-TILL TECHNIQUES

BELLA LINDE

PHOTOS BY LENA GRANEFELT

TRANSLATED BY GUN PENHOAT

Skyhorse Publishing

CONTENTS

FOREWORD

It is possible to garden without a spade.

I didn't quite believe my ears when I first heard about people gardening without digging the soil. Truth be told, I didn't think they were "all there"! It was evident to me that the garden tool shed ought to have at least one spade, and that a cultivated garden bed had to be dug both in the fall and spring. That's what I believed.

Nevertheless, the No-Dig idea did pique my interest. A combination of laziness and a constant hunger for knowledge, vegetables, and flowers made me head into the No-Dig gardening world. Such adventures waited for me! Crop failure, composting accidents, and horse manure incidents . . . to aha-moments, donated silage bales, cheering, and fantastic harvests! I was hooked!

Dig-free cultivating, which is known in everyday language as both "No-Dig" gardening and cover crop gardening, helps me produce vegetables and flowers today without having to lift one single shovelful of dirt. In addition to not being obligated to dig, the natural soil life is allowed to work in peace and establish the natural nutritional framework, which just about makes fertilizing redundant. Garden soil that is always covered maintains even levels of carbon. Furthermore, when I don't rummage around in the earth, carbon dioxide emissions are reduced. This makes both me and the method pretty climate smart.

Using the No-Dig method hasn't just been kind to my back, the environment, and my pocketbook; it has given me the pleasure of getting to know lots of interesting people, garden beds, and compost heaps.

I have talked to No-Dig gardeners all over the country, interviewed soil producers, and tormented experts with my never-ending questions. Communal composting facilities have been scrutinized, and cover crop material was ferreted around in. I visited with Börje Remstam, the Swedish Cover Crop King, in his hometown, Eskilstuna. Remstam hasn't gripped a spade since 1979. Books, blogs, and YouTube videos gave me loads of inspiration. A course with the No-Dig master Charles Dowding in Somerset, undoubtedly the most beautiful part of England, removed any lingering hesitation. I'll never buy another spade!

From Södermanland, Sweden,
during full gardening season,
Bella Linde

NO-DIG GARDENING—
THIS IS HOW IT'S DONE

To garden without first digging is just as easy as it sounds. The method is simple: you don't turn the soil over. The soil is also never left bare, rather it's replenished with layers of compost or covered with organic plant material. This cover helps the bed retain moisture and protects it against weather, wind, and nasty weeds. It also adds humus elements that make the soil both nutrient-rich and porous.

No-Dig gardening is not only about not disturbing the soil, it's also about adding new soil and humus in the form of composted or non-decomposed organic plant matter.

Put away the spade

Most people associate gardening with digging. We shift tons of dirt to aerate and loosen it; dig down manure and harvest plant debris; till weeds into the dark and uproot germinating weeds to kill them off. It's a Sisyphean task performed every fall and spring, accompanied by sweat and sore backs. Now this is totally unnecessary, and in fact, directly harmful.

The problem with digging is that it destroys the soil structure. First, the worms and small insects worked like mad to create humus and make tunnels for oxygen and water. Then, microorganisms freed up nutrition and wove together a subterranean network which, together with the plants, created a healthy growing environment—and then you arrive with a spade and turn it all upside down. Undesirably, carbon dioxide is also released when you dig. Admittedly, it might have a marginal effect on the carbon level in the ground . . . but still.

In short, the result of a No-Dig and a mulched/cover crop garden is that all the millions of microorganisms, worms, and other small crawlies living in the soil can work undisturbed. When the soil organisms' infrastructure is left in peace they can break down nutrients from organic and inorganic materials at a natural pace, transmitting them to hungry plants. This is profitable, not least for fungi. It's especially beneficial for mycelium which, in exchange for carbohydrates, transmits nutrients to plant roots. These roots are actually wrecked when you cut through the soil with your spade.

Gardeners have certainly dug soil through the ages with, admittedly, productive results. I'm not saying digging doesn't work. However, what is so good with No-Dig gardens is they can grow bigger and healthier crops than the dug ones. The British grower Charles Dowding proves this by, for example, regularly growing identical crops in both dug and non-dug soil. He has shown time after time the same result: crops grow well in dug soil, but even better in non-dug soil. By refusing to dig you're being kind toward both your body and the environment—and you're rewarded with healthy and fertile soil.

Never ever leave the soil bare
A vital detail of the No-Dig method is that you never, ever, leave the soil bare. This replicates how the ground looks out in nature. Nobody goes out there raking leaves or weeding. Fallen leaves, grasses, branches, and other plant matter provide a protective cover, and with the help of busy soil organisms, it's all converted into nutrient-rich humus. The roots of withered plants stay in the ground where they leave tunnels for oxygen and water, all the while decomposing into humus and nutrition.

If the garden beds are given compost or non-decayed organic matter regularly, the organisms in the soil get something to work with, converting it to humus and nutrients. The process gives the soil a balanced pH, which reduces the risk for diseases. When the microorganisms get hold of the cover material the result is a soil with a stronger immune system.

NO-DIG GARDENING IN A NUTSHELL

- Do not dig.
- Never leave the soil bare.
- Add cover material and/or compost.
- Keep the soil covered with living plant matter as much of the year as possible. This increases the photosynthesis and supports the microorganisms.
- Leave the roots in the soil when harvesting.
- Do not walk on and compact the soil.

ADVANTAGES OF NO-DIG GARDENING

- No digging
- Fewer weeds
- Less watering
- Porous soil
- Less need for fertilizer
- More worm fertilizer
- Even and natural nutrient circulation
- pH level is self-regulating
- Plants get stronger immune systems
- Increased yields
- Prevents flooding
- Drought hardy
- Binds carbon in the soil
- Prevents leaching of nutrients
- Time saver
- Simple
- Economical

The continual addition of plant material also builds up the planting area slightly above the surrounding ground level, aiding drainage and warming the soil earlier in spring. The mounded soil also retains heat over time. In addition, the cover/mulch material acts as a protective layer that maintains moisture, prevents weeds from taking hold, and evens out the ground temperature.

The principle of No-Dig gardening is to use two kinds of cover materials: the garden beds are amended with either completed compost or non-decomposed organic plant material which is allowed to compost directly on the beds. If No-Dig is the "body" of the No-Dig gardening method, the organic plant matter/mulch is its soul.

Climate smart and economical

Not only does No-Dig make gardening simpler for the gardener, it is also environmentally friendly. You create a good environment for subterranean life, and this is climate smart. Moreover, the increased humus helps bind atmospheric carbon, and to a certain extent helps counteract the emissions from the burning of fossil fuels.

MICROORGANISMS
Hidden organisms such as bacteria, virus, fungus, and protozoans are known under the collective term microorganisms or microbes.

The "4 per 1000" initiative was launched in 2015 at the climate conference in Paris, France. The initiative aspires to motivate more people to use agricultural practices that bind carbon in the soil. According to the initiative takers, if the global humus layer is increased by only 4 percent, it would strengthen fertility, simultaneously making up for the global increase of carbon dioxide emission caused by humanity. The suggested agricultural practices are regenerative (i.e. improving or renewing, building on the assumption that growers plant a diversity of crops over time within the same area, always have crops growing, disturb the soil as little as possible, never leave the soil bare, and always keep soil health as the focus). In other words, exactly what No-Dig Gardening is all about.

At the kitchen garden level, positive effects on the climate are achieved through a humus-rich soil which manages moisture

The soil is never left bare. Cover/mulch plant materials protect and add nutrients and humus elements.

retention and portions out nutrients evenly to hungry and thirsty plants, as opposed to leaching which causes excessive enrichment (eutrophication) of nearby water sources. The porous structure allows soil to easily absorb great quantities of water, protecting against flooding during heavy rains. The opposite applies too: in a drought, the healthy soil stays porous and well. Another ecological advantage is everything grown in the garden eventually can be used for mulch or building new garden beds, reducing trips to recycling facilities. Since the mulched plant matter breaks down into fine and nutrient-rich humus, it eliminates the need to purchase fertilizer and garden soil (especially those packaged in plastic bags). Premade garden soils contain large quantities of peat moss. Peat isn't just a limited resource; when harvested out of marshlands and bogs, it releases greenhouse gases. Mulch and compost gardening provide natural nutrition, strengthening the plants' immune systems. This helps eliminate the need to use artificial fertilizer or chemical pesticides and lessens the impact on the environment. Considering it all, a No-Dig garden is a win-win for both the environment and the pocketbook.

The role models

In our time, a few personalities stand out for having paved the way for No-Dig gardening. Ruth Stout, an American gardener, is one of them. By 1949 she had grown tired of plowing. Having pondered the fact that perennials return without the ground being manually prepared, she decided to try out annuals in No-Dig beds. She found an old forgotten overwintered pile of hay that had decayed into humus. Ruth's experimental method, coupled with the humus, gave her great results. Stout started writing articles enthusiastically promoting No-Dig gardening. She eventually published a book about mulched crops, *The Ruth Stout No-Work Garden,* a small mulched-bed gardening bible. A revised edition with the title *The Work-Free Garden* was published in Sweden in 1979. Börje Remstam, a Swede, working up a sweat trying to dig the uncooperative clay soil in Södermanland (a county near Stockholm), found her book. Börje successfully created a No-Dig and mulched garden using Stout's experience and insights. Börje

Remstam was for many years president of an organic-biological gardening association in Sweden. The association's motto is "For a healthy earth, healthy plants, healthy animals, and a healthy humanity." Its members strive to educate about ecological and biological cultivation. The membership newsletter has published many instructive articles about No-Dig gardening. In 2007, he published a personable and tip-filled book about mulched and covered bed gardening, in which the earthworm has a starring role.

Nils Åkerstedt, a gardener near Sundsvall, Sweden, was experimenting in the 1960s with gardening in grass cuttings and sand. He wrote about his experiment in the journal *Natur & Trädgård* and the subscribers soon started following his advice. In the 1980s Åkerstedt wrote a series of influential books about mulching, cultivation, gardening, and nature.

The English No-Dig gardener Charles Dowding was also inspired by Ruth Stout. Dowding was using the No-Dig method in 1983 to grow produce for sale at four market gardens. Dowding was featured in the garden program Gardener's World for the first time in 1988, becoming enormously popular as a spokesman for organic gardening. For Dowding, organic gardening was a given, but it was still regarded as a novelty by the public. Charles Dowding continues to be very public with his intense promotion of No-Dig gardening with beds he mulches using many different kinds of compost. He reaches out through many media sources: books, friendly blog posts, free newbie guides, in-person and online courses, informative calendars, and YouTube videos. There's no end to his shared knowledge, which he always presents with a slightly timid smile.

American microbiologist Dr. Elaine Ingham has had a big influence on No-Dig gardening. She defined the *soil food web* at the beginning of the 1980s. Since then, Ingham has diligently researched and illustrated how a good relationship between plants and soil microorganisms and small insects guarantees plants get the correct amount of nutrients at the right time. Elaine Ingham's view is that Mother Earth is smart and she has fine-tuned the method over the last billion years, and today's gardeners can just sit back and thank her.

LET'S GET STARTED!

When you are putting down new No-Dig garden beds there are several kinds to choose from: compost, lasagna, and hügel beds. Which one you choose depends on the location and your access to soil, compost, and different kinds of organic matter.

Once the garden beds are set down, you can choose between covered/mulched beds and compost beds. A mulched bed is refreshed continuously with new organic material that decomposes on the surface of the soil. A compost bed receives a thick layer of completed compost only once a year. A common reaction to the sight of the compost garden bed is that it looks bare. However, that is not the case because the compost itself is the cover material.

Compost gardening is advantageous if the garden has a lot of slugs. The slugs can hide under the plant matter in a mulched bed but they are more visible on a compost bed. In addition, the composted material is not quite as attractive to slugs as they are more likely to go for the organic plant matter on which they will munch with a hearty appetite.

CHANGE METHOD IN AN EXISTING VEGETABLE BED

You can turn any garden bed into a No-Dig bed immediately, even if you have already grown produce there. There is absolutely no need to redo everything. The only thing you need to do is start putting down organic plant matter on your existing vegetable bed. Composted or non-decomposed material, it makes no difference. The important thing is to continually cover the bed with new organic material. It will take a few years for the soil and its inhabitants to get used to the new method, but that doesn't mean that you have to wait. You can absolutely practice No-Dig gardening right away!

LAYING DOWN NO-DIG BEDS

It is ridiculously simple and fast to construct garden beds using the No-Dig gardening method! Within a few hours you can build a No-Dig bed if you have all the materials at hand.

Vegetables need weed-free and nutritious soil. That's the reason why much of the preparation is about smothering weeds, especially the perennial weed roots that lurk under the soil surface.

Regardless of whether you are using the mulch or compost method, you'll start by covering the designated area with a thick layer of newspapers or cardboard to suffocate any grass and weeds. The cardboard/paper material decomposes gradually, leaving the soil weed-free with a good depth under the bed. The soil's organisms will work upwards, loosening the soil and breaking down the compost or mulching material, releasing nutrients.

Once the smothering material is in place it's time to add the organic plant material, which also works as a weed killer. Although there are different ways to do this, it basically works by building up the garden bed in layers. A lasagna bed is a garden bed built in several layers from different materials. A garden bed using only compost is called a compost bed. As a rule, this type is only given a thick layer of compost on the surface. However, if the compost is in different stages of decay, the coarser pieces should be on the bottom and finer on the upper layer. (Precise instructions on how to build the different garden beds can be found on p. 25–30.)

It's wise to lay down the beds in fall. That way they have time to settle over winter and be ready for use in the spring. Of course, that doesn't mean that you can't start them in spring just before you want to use them. In that case, they won't have had time to settle so it might be necessary to add some extra planting soil or finely decomposed compost to sow and plant in. Material which isn't broken down properly won't retain moisture well, so spring-started No-Dig garden beds need careful watering.

A new bed is thus usable the first year but will function best beginning in its third year because the natural nutritional cycle will then be working properly.

It is good to take your time planning and laying out the bed, especially the smothering of weeds and the cleanup all around the planting area. It makes everything so much easier if the bedding material and tools are in the right place at the start. The work that follows will be more enjoyable. It's easy to both compost and add to the mulch cover on the bed if a composting bin and the collected mulching materials are in close proximity to the garden. It's also wise to place a garden bed near the kitchen in order to have the crops within reach.

No plans or plantings are ever set in stone. Gardening changes in conjunction with how your interests develop and with new knowledge and discoveries. When and how often you spend time in your kitchen garden are also important factors. However, if there is one decision most No-Dig gardeners are happy to stick with for the long-term, it's this: that the spade stays in the shed.

Planning and placement

- Most vegetables demand at least eight (8) hours of sunlight a day. A good placement for the garden bed is with the shortest side facing the south; that way you'll profit from both morning and evening sun.
- Vegetables need regular care, so place the kitchen garden as near the house and the entrance as possible. If your path of travel is always by the garden bed you're more likely to discover and eliminate potential pests and diseases before they take hold. If you place the bed near the kitchen you don't have to go far to get your daily harvest.
- The garden bed needs to be protected from strong winds. The wind lowers the temperature, which is especially noticeable in the spring.
- Garden beds in windy locations can be protected by planks, a trellis, walls, and/or hedges. Some wind is not a problem, it can sometimes help blow off some of the possible insect pests.
- Choose a garden bed location without trees nearby. Tree canopies shade the crop and tree roots steal moisture and can grow into the garden bed. If you have to place your garden bed

near an area with trees, each year cut through the ground with a sharp spade (this is an exception) to slice through the roots that steal nutrients and humidity. Regularly prune trees and hedges growing too close.

- The simplest way to begin is by building a No-Dig bed in an already existing garden bed or on top of a lawn area, as you can profit from the already existing soil.
- It is wiser to dig out (yes, another exception) terrace steps if the garden bed is to be located on a steep slope. This is hard work during the lay-out phase, but you're rewarded with a more easily accessed and managed garden than if you have to slip and slide on a sloping hill.
- Plan on putting 17" (50 cm) -wide paths between the beds; they will stop grass and weeds and give you enough space to reach into the beds from all sides.

Prepare the ground

Before laying out the bed, remove as many stones as possible to give root vegetables free space. A ground that is heavily compacted from heavy machinery or vehicles will need to be aerated. Stick a pitchfork into the ground and move it back and forward to ease the pressure and to let in air. Do not turn the soil over because that will disturb the subterranean life. Instead, amend with organic plant material to give the soil inhabitants a hand in reestablishing the structural balance.

THEY ALL NEED LIGHT!
When planning your crops, consider the orientation and the height of the plants. Tall plants should be to the north, shorter plants to the south, and the in-betweens in falling range. That way the small plants avoid being shaded by the tall and everybody gets the necessary light.

A heavily weed-infested area will require at least three (3) mowings before you lay down a bed. Compost or dry the clippings and use them later on for mulching.

Do you have moss in your lawn? As a rule, you can lay down a bed directly on the moss; the moss will die under a thick soil bed, and it decomposes just like peat. However, moss is difficult to break down, taking a long time to decompose. If you're concerned the moss won't break

down within a reasonable time span, rip it up and compost it on the side in a warm compost pile. (Read more about warm compost on p. 106.)

If the soil is full of stubborn weed roots—for example, dandelions—you should remove them before laying out your bed. Push in a small digging fork and loosen the root carefully by moving it back and forth. Try to get the roots out as intact as possible as every little bit left over can be the beginning of a new weed. Compost the roots.

If the ground is really heavily infested with nasty root weeds, like ground elder or quackgrass, you may need to cover the area for a few years with plastic sheeting or a tarpaulin. The look is unattractive and it takes patience, but by not letting in the slightest ray of light you will starve out the weeds. One way to improve the appearance is to cover and hide the plastic with wood shavings or something similar. You can also build temporary garden beds on top of the plastic and grow plants that don't have deep roots. The material from the temporary beds goes into building the permanent beds once the plastic is removed.

Gardening in pallet collars or pots could be a solution if the ground is covered in asphalt or concrete, or if there is a risk that the soil is contaminated. Place the pallet collar on top of a pallet that is covered with a ground cloth. Admittedly, there isn't quite the same benefit from life in the soil as a garden bed on the ground, but it's far better than not being able to grow anything at all.

ROTARY TILLER = A NO-NO!

Using a rotary tiller to break up soil is as bad for microorganisms as using a spade. You'll only shoot yourself in the foot. Of course, the result from a rotary tiller will be a patch of loosened soil, but at the same time, the churning results in a great many bits of grass and weed roots being flung about. Once all those start growing again you'll need to attack with the tiller, which will spread more roots, which will start growing and . . .

Skip the tiller and instead create a garden bed by covering the soil with cardboard. The bed itself functions as a smothering cover later on.

REFUSE TO DIG IN CLAY SOIL!

Common belief is that clay soil has to be dug to be aerated and loosened up, but in No-Dig gardening that is obviously not on the agenda. All soils are seen as assets here, which means they are amended with as much organic plant matter as possible. Compost and mulching material attracts worms and other crawlies that will dig tunnels and create good quality texture out of even the most awkward soils. Set aside the shovel and a clay soil can become well-fed and porous in only a few years.

NASTY WEEDS

There are two (2) kinds of weeds: the ones that spread by seeds and the ones that spread by runners (roots).

Seed weeds are usually annual. They spread by seeds that land on the soil and germinate. Due to their shallow roots these weeds are typically easy to remove. They can also be smothered with a cover of a solid material.

A few examples of weeds that spread by seed: Mouse-Ear Cress, False Chamomile, Shepherd's Purse, Spotted Dead-Nettle, Lamb's Quarters, Chickweed, Wild Mustard.

Weeds spread by runners are perennials and they spread both by roots and seeds. If even a small piece of the root system is left in the ground the weed is likely to survive. The real noxious weeds spread through the soil with root stock or extensive root tangles. The most persistent weeds might need several years of complete covering with black plastic to be eliminated.

Examples of weeds with runners: Ground Elder (Bishop's Weed), Quackgrass, Creeping Bellflower, Dandelion, Creeping Buttercup, Nettle, Field Bindweed.

Prepare the base of the garden bed

- Measure out the crop-growing area you want. A few examples:

  A 4' x 13' bed (120 cm x 400 cm) will provide a good crop-growing area, but not so big that you can't easily reach into the middle from both sides. It is also short enough to walk around with ease without having to step into the crop area.

  A bed measuring 2½' x 23' (75 cm x 700 cm) will provide an excellent crop row and is narrow enough to step over without trampling the growing area.

- Cover the base with two to three layers of cardboard or a thick layer of newspaper. If using newspaper, place at least three layers unfolded on top of each other. It's best to remove all tape and preferably all staples. Place the paper material on the soil so it covers the growing area and leave a 20" (50 cm) -wide path all around and in between the beds. Make a larger covered base and you'll avoid weeds creeping into the crop area. Add cover materials to avoid messy paths. Paths between the beds allow for room to move a wheelbarrow. The paper materials must overlap; you can't allow the slightest ray of light to peek in.

- Create the shape. The most practical way to delineate a rectangular No-Dig bed is to use four dowels and a long piece of string. Measure out your desired size, place a dowel in each corner, and loop and tighten the string around the dowels so the bed shape is clearly visible. A water hose is an excellent tool for making curved shapes. Place the hose in the desired shape and build the garden bed inside the contour.

You now have the base for one of the following beds:

Preparation of a compost bed

Compost bed

A compost bed consists of a thick layer of garden compost, kitchen compost, leaf or livestock compost, or a mixture of several kinds. Be extra careful if using livestock compost when you're preparing your garden bed in the spring. It needs to be composted twice (fully processed) and decomposed for you to be able to plant in it. (Read more about the stages farmyard compost goes through on p. 113.)

- Place a 6" to 8" (15 cm to 20 cm) layer of compost on top of the paper material covering the measured garden bed. If you have limited access to fully processed compost, build the bed with, for example, 2" to 2½" (5 cm to 6 cm) of partly processed livestock compost in the bottom, 2" to 2½" (5 cm to 6 cm) partly composted garden compost in the middle, and 2" to 2½" (5 cm to 6 cm) of fully processed compost as top layer. The bottom layer will continue to compost in place in the bed.

- Pat or step lightly on the compost to pack it into a secure planting bed. Water. If you are doing this in the spring your bed is now ready for planting.
- If you are preparing your garden bed in the fall, it needs to be covered by a dark garden fabric, straw, grass, or leaves before winter sets in. The material lets in humidity but not light, so weeds won't grow. The compost will have broken down further into fine humus when you remove the protective cover in the spring. Weeds and any lawn underneath usually will have died off and decomposed by now. A lawn might take a bit longer, but the process has started and you can still plant a crop.

Lasagna bed

A lasagna bed consists of a variety of organic matter layered like a dish of lasagna. The material is composted gradually while in place, which results in a humus-rich, nutrient-rich, and warm garden bed.

- Place a big bunch of branches, twigs and/or wood chips, and other garden debris on top of the cardboard or newspaper covering the measured base of the garden bed.
- Fill up with everything from plant debris, seaweed, and grass cuttings to pulled weeds and leaves. If you shred the leaves with a lawn mower they will decompose faster. Make the layers 2" to 4" (5 cm to 10 cm) thick. You can never have too much material, and as long as it isn't too coarse it doesn't matter in which order you stack the layers. Water in between layers. It's good to finish with a 2" to 10" (5 cm to 10 cm) layer of fine crumbly garden compost and/or fully processed livestock compost. Water.
- If you built this in the spring the lasagna bed is now ready for planting. However, because the material isn't broken down yet, you'll want to place narrow rows of soil to sow in and also make small holes for plants. Use bagged commercial garden

Preparation of a lasagna bed

soil, soil collected from another area in the garden, fine crumbly garden compost, or thoroughly processed livestock compost.

- If you prepare the bed in the fall, cover it for the winter with straw, leaves, grass, or a dark garden cloth. The material lets humidity in but not light, therefore inhibiting weed growth. When you remove the protective cover in the spring the organic matter will be decomposing. Any grass and weeds underneath will be smothered and decomposed. A section of lawn may take a bit longer to decompose but you can still start a crop where the decomposing has started. If the material is too coarse you may have to place rows of soil to sow in, or make small holes with garden soil for plants to go in. Use bagged commercial garden soil, soil from another part of the garden, or thoroughly processed livestock manure compost.

Special Section:

Hügel bed

A hügel bed is a raised garden bed with a base of logs covered with twigs and garden debris, soil, and/or compost. The logs provide a lengthy decomposition process, which improves the soil's fertility and ability to retain humidity, and helps the bed warm up earlier in the spring—all to the advantage of the crop that is going to grow on top. *Hügel* is German for a hill or mound.

Preparation:

- Place a number of logs side-by-side on top of the paper material to cover the base of the planned garden bed. The logs can be even in length or smaller pieces added together to fit. A few slight gaps between the logs won't matter. You can also place smaller stumps together with the cut surface facing up. Fill the spaces with twigs, bark, leaves, pine needles and, if you have it, compost. Tamp/tramp down the material, then water.

- Add a second layer of logs or stumps if you want to. Fill the spaces with garden debris and then water.

- Place branches and twigs over the logs. Fill with plant matter like leaves, straw, hay, ensilage, compost, seaweed, and fresh grass cuttings if you have any available. Make 2" to 4" (5 cm to 10 cm) -thick layers. You can't have too much material and it doesn't matter in which order you place it as long as it is not too coarse. Tamp/tramp down the bed in between layers to stabilize the bed. Water.

- Cover the whole hügel bed with a 4" (10 cm) compost layer, garden soil, or soil from another part of the garden and make sure that it is free of weeds and stones. Tamp down and then water. If you build the bed in the spring it will be ready for use.

LOGS TO USE

You can use any kind of tree trunks, logs, or stumps for the bottom layer of a hügel bed but the most desirable varieties are alder, poplar, apple, and birch. Scots pine and spruce work too. However, fresh conifer wood might still contain terpenes (i.e. aromatic compounds in concentrated form, which might be harmful for humans). The terpenes will have leached out of pine trees that have been dead for several years.

Preparation of a hügel bed

- If you prepare the bed in the fall, cover it with straw, leaves, grass, or a dark garden cloth to protect it over winter. The material will let humidity through but not light, and this will inhibit weed growth as a result.
- When you remove the cover in spring, weeds and possibly lawn turf under the bed will have decomposed. A slow decomposing process is happening inside the bed. If the material isn't sufficiently decomposed you may have to add rows of planting soil to sow in, or make small holes in the soil for the plants to go in. Use bagged commercial soil, soil collected from another part of the garden, or fully processed livestock compost.

Pallet collar—a smaller-sized No-Dig bed

A pallet collar is an approximately 8" (20 cm) -tall wood frame with the standard measurement 3'11" x 2'⅓" (120 cm x 80 cm). They were originally made to transport goods. The frames can be placed on top of each other to create flexible boxes; this has made them incredibly popular for use as raised beds.

Obviously, it is possible to make a No-Dig bed in a pallet collar. All three beds–lasagna, compost, and hügel–work great. Naturally, the soil dries out quicker in the limited space of the pallet collar so it will need more frequent watering than a larger garden bed.

There are now pallet collars made especially for raised beds available at home improvement stores and plant nurseries. Sometimes it is possible to find discarded pallet collars for free in industrial zones or on building sites. Don't use collars made from treated lumber because they can leach toxins into the garden bed.

Weed-free paths

To cut down on weeds in the paths between the beds it is sometimes necessary to cover the paths with a thick and smothering polypropylene (PP) ground cloth, which is then covered with straw, wood chips, or other material that is comfortable to walk on. The cloth needs to be highly opaque (i.e. let through extremely little light). The advantage with a cloth is that it lets through water. The disadvantage is that the occasional aggressive weed can get through; however, it is very simple to

remove them by hand. Warning! Do not use common tarpaulin—
the water won't run through the dense fabric, only pool in the
pathways. Tarpaulin also tears over time and you will suddenly find
pieces of plastic fluttering about in the garden.

You can just use cardboard to cover the paths, although that
means a bit more work. First, you'll need to put down at least two
layers. Second, you will probably need to renew the cardboard
occasionally. To do this, any covering of wood chips or straw
would need to be removed and then be put back again on the new
cardboard.

Note: Never make a garden bed base out of ground cloth,
unless it is biodegradable. The cloth will act as a barrier for the
microorganisms, and plastic material isn't really suitable in a
kitchen garden.

POTATOES—THE PERFECT GROUND BREAKER

Potato plants are efficient
and simple for an initial crop
in a garden because the
roots penetrate, break up,
and loosen the soil. To plant
potatoes:

• Place overlapping
cardboard or thick layers of
newspaper over the proposed
growing area. Do not leave
any gaps between boards or
papers.

• Place potatoes on the
paper material. Space them at
10" to 1' apart (25 cm–30 cm).
Water.

• Cover the potatoes with a
thick layer of straw—at least
1' (30 cm). Water.

   The potatoes can root once
the paper has disintegrated.

• Check the vegetative
growth and water as needed.
This is extra important during
dry summers.

• Gradually "hill" by adding
straw or other cover material.
Never expose the growing
potato to light because it will
turn green and become toxic.

• You can harvest by putting
your hand down into the
cover material once the potato
plant has flowered.

• The following year the
garden bed is weed free and
porous and ready for new
crops. Don't grow potatoes in
the same patch for the next
three (3) to four (4) years due
to the risk of wireworms. (You
can read more about wire-
worms and how to get rid of
them on p. 199.)

	COMPOST NO-DIG GARDENING	MULCHED MATERIAL NO-DIG GARDENING
PROS	+ Healthier soil. + Composted humus feeds and provides the soil with long-term nutrition. A continuous stream of material is provided for worms, small insects, and microorganisms to work with. + The material is porous, making it easy to remove weed runners and seed weeds from the surface. + You can sow and plant into the compost. + Compost warms up early in the spring and holds the warmth longer into the fall, which extends the growing season. + Less space makes it easier to spot damage. Fewer diseases and pests. + Not as attractive as mulched beds to slugs. It's easier to spot the ones that do venture in. + The garden beds look neat and tidy. + Retains humidity and doesn't require a lot of watering. + Reduced need for topping up with fertilizer. The nutrients are released slowly and are available when the plants need them. + The worms loosen the soil and fertilize it with their excrement. + Reduces weeds. + The material binds carbon in the soil.	+ Healthier soil. + The cover material provides continually decomposing material, which provides the soil with humus and long-term nutrition. It provides a continuous stream of material for worms, small insects, and microorganisms to consume. + Reduced need for topping up with fertilizer. The nutrients are released slowly and are available when the plants need them. + Retains humidity and doesn't require a lot of watering. + The worms loosen the soil and fertilize it with their excrement. + Reduces weeds. + The plant matter doesn't have to go through the compost bin, resulting in less labor. + The material binds carbon in the soil.
CONS	- The cover material has to be processed through the composting bin, which means more physical work. - Some compost is nutrient poor. - A badly working compost pile doesn't reach the heat needed to kill diseases and weed seeds. If this compost is spread across the garden the diseases and weeds are spread, too.	- The cover material insulates, preventing the soil from warming up in spring. The cover needs to be pushed aside for sowing and planting crops. - If the cover is positioned improperly it risks smothering seeds and small plants. - The cover material may make the garden bed look messy. - Might be difficult finding enough mulching material. - Birds may root around in mulch. - Slugs like to hide under mulch.

HÜGEL BED

+ Healthier soil.
+ The cover material is continually decomposing compost material, which feeds and provides the soil with long-term nutrition. It provides a continuous stream of material for worms, small insects, and microorganisms to work with.
+ Breakdown of logs and branches happens gradually, which provides a steady stream of nutrients.
+ Logs and branches absorb and store rainwater and release it during drier periods.
+ The wood generates heat when decomposing, which provides a slightly earlier start to the growing season, and the possibility to grow heat-loving plants.
+ The soil is automatically aerated when logs and branches break down.
+ Decomposing logs are a favorite food for small insects and microorganisms, which results in viable sustainable growing soil.
+ A raised bed is ergonomically correct.
+ The material binds carbon in the soil.

- Crops with deep roots cannot be planted the first years before woody material has properly started breaking down. The woody material stops plant roots' growth.
- Wood is carbon-rich and can steal nitrogen during decomposition.
- The bed height is reduced as the material decomposes.

PAPER—A WORM FAVORITE

Worms love paper and happily drag it into the soil. Use brown cardboard with as little print on it as possible. Corrugated cardboard is for sale in building supply stores if you can't find any free boxes. Cardboard is usually placed in the bottom of the garden bed but it can also be used to cover plant material in the winter, or as ground cover when you make holes for plants in the material underneath. You'll need to weigh down the cardboard placed on top or it will blow away.

SO, WHAT *IS* SOIL?

For today's gardener, soil is most commonly available bagged at plant nurseries or grocery stores. Commercially bagged soil is not at all obligatory. A normal garden usually has enough existing soil that is amendable with organic plant matter: grass cuttings, garden debris, harvest leftovers, withered leaves, and compost at different stages of processing. The subterranean microorganisms work this material and turn it into nutrient-rich humus. Peat is the main component in bagged soil sold commercially. Actually, peat is more a substrate than a soil, if we check the mineral content. It is an excellent soil amendment but its use is becoming problematic. First, regeneration is very slow, which puts peat into the finite resource category. Second, peat harvesting releases carbon dioxide, which adds to the greenhouse effect. One of peat's advantages is that it's usually weed free, and it is good for sowing in.

Soil is never used up, at least not as long as you care for and amend it. That means you never have to change soil in a garden bed or pallet collar. The important thing here is to amend the soil (i.e. make sure that the garden bed is continually fed compost and mulched with organic plant matter that can be worked on by the microorganisms).

FRAMED!

If you want to frame your garden bed with some timber, it's a good idea to place the frame on the cardboard/paper base before you add the organic material. The frame will contain the soil and compost, making the bed look neat and tidy. This is, of course, not a necessity for gardening. If your garden has Spanish slugs, a frame might even be very unwise; the slugs will move in and hide underneath the timber, depositing their eggs in any small cavity.

Well-cared-for tools are priceless. The following are some tools that are handy to have for your No-Dig gardening. It's totally unnecessary to run out and buy them all at once. Many can be borrowed from or shared with other gardeners.

Good-to-have equipment for No-Dig gardening

Shovel. Moves material like sand, gravel, and fine soil.

Pitch fork. Fork with narrow tines that is used to lift grass, leaves, compost, and manure.

Digging fork. Fork with wide tines that is used to loosen soil. Also used to turn and empty compost.

Broadfork. A broader fork with two (2) handles and several deep-penetrating sharp tines. It loosens and aerates the soil. Used both to prepare garden beds and to lift root vegetables at harvest. They come in different widths, with four (4) to seven (7) tines. This is sometimes called a u-hand digger. Saves your back.

Ground rake. For leveling sown garden beds, collecting clods and stones, and to rake in broadcast seeds. The reverse side can be used for breaking off/pushing weeds.

Rakes. Rake together grass and leaves. Manual hay rake collects hay and long grass. A leaf rake collects short grass and leaves.

Screen. Separates larger pieces of matter from compost and sand.

Electrical/motorized lawn mower with bagger. Simplifies grass cutting and collection of grass cuttings for cover material.

Scythe. A curved sharp blade attached to a long shaft with 1 or 2 short handles. Used for cutting long grasses and plants along, for example, ditches or road shoulders.

Soil thermometer. Measures the soil temperature and is handy for the spring bed sowing. Some seeds rot if the ground is too cold.

Compost thermometer. Measures temperature in the compost pile. It is made from stainless steel and has a long probe.

Dibber. This is a planting tool. It makes holes in the soil for sowing seeds or small plants. Often made of wood, it sometimes has measurements marked along the probe to ensure proper planting depth. Plant nurseries sell mainly short, thin dibbers for planting seeds. You need to kneel on the ground to use this. You can stand upright to make the plant holes with a longer and sturdier dibber, something which both protects your back and is also more efficient. Make your own dibber from a spade handle. Remove the spade blade and hone the end of the handle until it is slightly rounded.

Weed hoe. A long-handled tool to remove weeds. There are several kinds, for example: Dutch hoe, Stirrup (action) hoe, garden weeding hoe. A Dutch hoe is also useful for turning soil, when soil needs to be pushed (hilled) against potatoes or other plants for protection or support.

Cultivator. A claw-like tool to loosen the soil surface and break up clods. Long or short handles.

Hand hoe. A short tool for weeding close to plants without damaging roots.

Garden claw rake. Small claw-like tool for loosening small soil areas and places where it is difficult to reach with a normal-sized garden hoe.

Daisy weeder. A narrow two-pronged tool for fully uprooting long-rooted weeds.

Secateur (shears). Tool for cutting off thinner branches and twigs. Prunes bushes and trees.

Hand Axe. Used for chopping off small branches and twigs from trees. Good for making sharp points on supports, wooden poles, and fences.

Knife. Used for trimming plants and for harvesting.

Scissors. For cutting, for example, string and slugs.

Buckets. For water, sand, compost, stones, weeds, soil. . . . There is always something that needs to be collected and carried away.

A dibber makes good planting holes in the soil.

Wheelbarrow. To transport larger amounts of garden material.

String. To bind up tall-growing or climbing plants and to lay down straight lines before sowing.

Landscape fabric, mat. Plastic cloth that smothers weeds. Often woven to allow water to freely soak through. It's mainly put down on paths and then covered with wood chips, bark or straw. You can also get an agro textile ground fabric that is compostable and biodegradable, which begins decomposing after three (3) years.

Non-woven fabric. Preserves the soil's warmth in early sowing. Protects the soil and crops from pests and extends the growing season. Preserves moisture in the soil. Exists in several thicknesses; the thicker fabrics last longer but are heavier with rainfall. An alternative is a closely woven, washable lace curtain.

Insects barrier. Fine mesh polyethylene. Protects the crop from cabbage root fly, carrot fly, and cabbage butterfly. Protects somewhat against flea beetles. A tightly woven lace curtain would do the trick.

Ground cover/weed barrier. A geotextile fabric. Used to cover the garden bed before sowing and after harvest to prevent weeds. Can also be used as a weed barrier in the beds during growing season; planting is then done through the fabric.

Compost wire panel. Really meant for garden compost bins but the compost dries out too easily in a wire bin. However, it is great to place on top of mulching material that might otherwise blow away. Also protects against roving pets and pests that can damage the beds.

Pots. Small pots for growing seedlings and larger for potting up later. The plants will grow in these before they are moved to the garden bed.

Paper pot maker. This is a wooden cylinder used as a mold for the fabrication of paper pots (i.e. pots made out of newspaper). This is a cheap and environmentally friendly method and is also kind to fragile plant roots. The plants are set in the bed, pots and all, and the pots decompose after planting.

Planting cells/greenhouse. A collection of sowing cells in molded plastic. Each cell has a hole in the bottom. The plant can easily be pushed up and out of the cell at potting up time or for planting in the bed. The cell molds come in different sizes from 35 to 150 cells per mold, and they also come in different depths. Different plants develop at different speeds and have different needs for water, so it is practical to choose molds with fewer cells and sow similar plants together. Choose deeper cells for plants with larger root systems like beans and cucumber plants. Go for molds in heavy plastic so they can be reused for years.

Sowing box. A deep tray for broadcast seeding where the seeds are not sown in individual pots or cells. The trays are available in plant nurseries but you can just as easily use plastic containers that once held fresh produce, empty glass containers, takeout containers, or similar items.

Seed planting dibber. A small wooden dowel that will help with sowing seeds and potting up small plants. It has a pointy end for making holes in the soil, and a blunt one to use to tamp down the soil after planting. The blunt end is also good for pushing the plant out of the pot from underneath so you don't damage the root system.

Watering can/water hose. A sprinkler head is a must for seeded areas.

Choose the right tools

Quality equipment is the be-all and end-all for your gardening, so always buy the best quality you can afford. Some advice:

- Get pots, trays, and seeding cells that can be used for many years.
- Avoid tools with plastic handles and fastenings. Check that connections and fastenings are robust.
- Buy tools that can be repaired so they don't have to be discarded if something wears out or breaks.
- Make sure that the lengths on forks and various rakes are meant for your height—it is awful trying to use tools with too short or too long handles.
- Check out second-hand stores. Old tools are usually of high quality and sometimes it's worth the time and sweat to clean, polish, fine-tune, and oil older tools.

NO-DIG GARDENING
METHOD APPLIED

Whether you garden with compost or non-decomposed organic plant matter, the basic principle is the same: from the season's first indoor-started plant to the last crop harvest, it's all about never putting a spade in the soil. The plants have the best prospects for healthy growth without being bothered by diseases and pests in a fertile, non-dug soil.

INDOOR SEED STARTING— START EARLY AND CONTINUE A LONG TIME

In climates with short growing seasons, you'll need to pre-cultivate certain plants (i.e. start seeds indoors in winter). Vegetables that need a long time to develop will not have time to mature if they are direct seeded in the garden beds in spring. Seeding them indoors gives them a leg up. Check with other local gardeners or look online to find out when you'll need to start your seeds. In some places, by February it's already time to start sowing seed trays with artichokes, chili peppers, bell peppers, leeks, and onions. Tomatoes, pumpkins, squash, cucumbers, and some cabbage varieties follow those.

It is important not to plant your seeds indoors too early. It is incredibly annoying to have a house full of plants you can't get into the garden beds.

BUT YOU'RE *OF COURSE* ALLOWED TO TOUCH THE SOIL!
No-Dig is not the same as not ever being allowed to touch the soil. Undisturbed is best. However, you have to touch the soil with a rake and cultivator, make rows for sowing and divets and holes when you plant, and then again at harvesting. And there's no way around it—to plant those perennials with their large root balls you'll probably *have* to dig.

ADDITIONAL LIGHT SOURCE

If indoor seeding/pre-cultivation starts early in the season, the days are short where you live, or you're seeding in a dark room, you'll need an extra light source in order to force plants and also prevent the plants from growing leggy. Plant nurseries sell grow lights, but common fluorescent lights attached above the seed trays work just as well. The lights need to be adjustable and should hang approximately 4–6 in. (10–15 cm) above the plants. If the lights are closer, you'll risk burning the plants. Even if your seed tray is on the window ledge, you might want to add grow lights to be sure your plants grow green and stout.

For most plants, you need to wait until the danger of the last frost is past before you direct sow in the garden bed. Depending on where you live, this may mean planting at the end of May, or even beginning of June. In some places, you can start much earlier. Check online or ask local gardeners.

An added advantage of starting plants indoors is that the plants are strong and hardy by the time they are ready for transplanting. This provides them with good odds against both pests and any diseases lurking in the growing area.

Pre-cultivation—how to do it:

- Pour soil or compost into a pot, seed tray, or sowing box. It is often recommended to use special porous, nutrient-poor planting soil for seed starting. However, it is becoming more usual to pre-cultivate in common planting soil or fully processed compost, going by the principle that when seeds are direct-sown in garden beds they never need any special soil, growing just fine where they are sown. Use small pots and cells, approximately 1¼ in. x 1¼ in. (3 cm x 3 cm), giving the soil a chance to dry out between watering.

- Water before sowing. Push the seeds down to the depth specified on the seed packet. Water as needed once more, but do this carefully so as not to disturb the seeds.

- Place the containers on a tray to make it possible to water from below. Cover with a clear plastic cover or plastic wrap and pierce air holes in this. Now the soil can breathe and the seeds won't rot in wet soil or dry out too much. Water regularly and always from below. It saves time and provides an even distribution. The soil should be damp but never soaking wet.

- Place the tray in a window or under grow lights once the seeds have germinated and the first leaves, the cotyledons, appear. The plants need 12 to 14 hours of light within a 24-hour period to grow sturdy instead of

BUY OR JOIN A PLANT EXCHANGE

Keeping in mind the cost of seeds, as well as the time and space needed to start plants indoors, it might be worth it to buy individual starters or join a plant exchange to get plants, especially the ones you don't need so many of.

TIP: TOMATOES
Lanky-looking tomatoes?
Remove all excess leaves,
leave off watering for a few
days, and then carefully push
the soft plant stem deep down
into the soil, leaving only the
tip sticking up. The plant will
develop roots along the length
of the stem, stabilizing the
plant. Soon the plant will be
pushing healthily above the
soil.

long and leggy. However, they need to rest at night. To stop the plants from growing too fast the temperature has to stay below 64.4°F (18°C).

- It's time to up-pot the plant (i.e. move the plant into a bigger pot with compost or planting soil, when the first true leaves appear and you can see roots at the bottom of the container. Don't use a pot that's too big—small plants risk rotting if they're in too much soil, especially if the soil is too wet. Plants will also develop a looser root system if they are planted directly in a large pot. Water. Place the pot in the window under grow lights. The early seeded plants usually need a second up-potting for the roots to develop properly.
- Starting a few weeks after the last up-potting, the plants also need some liquid fertilizer once a week. (Read more about liquid fertilizer on p. 121.) Quick growers that are planted later in peat pellets or cells seldom need to be repotted; they can go directly into the garden beds when the soil has warmed.

(Read more about liquid fertilizer on p. 121.)

RIGHT TIME FOR INDOOR SEED STARTING
January–February: Eggplant, artichoke
February–March: Chili peppers, bell peppers
March–April: Tomato, cauliflower, broccoli, kale, Tuscan kale, white cabbage, red and yellow onions, leeks
May: Cucumber, squash, pumpkin (+/- a few weeks depending on your location)

ONION SETS
Onions grown from seed need to be pre-cultivated. Plant nurseries also sell pre-cultivated onion sets. Only plant heat-treated sets as they won't bolt in the garden bed. A dry root clump cannot easily absorb water from the surrounding soil and the plant risks drying out or wilting.

Setting out the plants

It is time to set out the pre-cultivated plants in the garden beds once the risk for frost has passed. You still need to look after the plants both before they go into the soil, and also after.

- **Hardening off.** Move the plants outside for a few hours each day for one week to let them get used to outside conditions. They need time to adjust to the wind and the sun's rays, not just the temperature difference. Move the plants back inside for the night. A shortcut is to leave them outside in a protected spot, controlling temperature and strong sunshine with the help of a floating row cover.

PLANTS THAT NEED TO BE STARTED INDOORS/PRE-CULTIVATED

If you live in a place with a shorter growing season (around 120 days or less), these plants need to be pre-cultivated to have a chance to mature in the garden before the season is over:

- Eggplant, chili peppers, bell peppers
- Onions, leeks
- Cardoons, artichokes
- Celeriac, celery
- Cucumbers, melons
- Cauliflower

PLANTS THAT CAN BE PRE-CULTIVATED OR DIRECT SOWN

If you live in a place with a shorter growing season (around 120 days or less), these plants are preferably started indoors but can be directly sown.

- Broccoli, Brussels sprouts, red and white cabbage, kale, Tuscan cabbage/kale, Savoy cabbage, oxheart cabbage
- Fennel, parsley
- Corn
- Pumpkin, squash
- Spring onions
- New Zealand spinach
- Peas, beans

- **Water.** Water the root clump before you place the plant.
- **Planting.** Make a hole that is large enough to accommodate the plant but not larger than is necessary. Use a dibber (i.e. a hole maker) to make sturdy holes. Just move the cover out of the way in a mulched bed and add handfuls of soil or well-ripened compost to the hole. Water the hole. Big plants may require that you make a hole through any remaining paper material. Place the plant in the hole, or separate broadcast seed plants and plant them individually or in clusters. (Read more about distance between plants and about cluster planting on p. 74–76.) Cover with compost or soil and tamp down to make sure the plant stands firmly. Water around the root clump. Replace the mulch around the plants. Handle the small plants carefully as they risk getting smothered if they end up under the mulch. Keep aside a few plants to plant later in case some of them don't take at first.
- **Water.** Additional watering around the roots of each plant spreads the soil carefully. It makes the roots search downwards into the soil instead of out toward the edge of the bed. Water each plant again after two days. Repeat watering in another two days if the soil feels dry. The plants should by now be in contact with the soil's nutritional network and be able to get at the humidity on their own.
- **Check the temperature.** Night frost is unpredictable. Keep an eye on the weather forecast and be prepared to put down floating row covers to protect the plants that are already planted in the garden bed.

Planting through a weed-blocking fabric

If your garden bed is invaded by lots of runner weeds, or if you're using perennial weeds for mulching material, help can come in the form of a weed-blocking ground fabric. The fabric smothers the weeds while letting air and water through, letting the plants grow in peace. Cut an "x" in the fabric, make a hole in the plant matter underneath, and put in the plant. Add soil or compost to the hole if the mulch isn't completely broken down. It can get really hot in the sun because the cloth is either brown or black. It's best to cover with another mulch like straw to protect from the heat.

Don't use a woven polypropylene ground cloth if you want to plant through it. As soon as this cloth is cut it will unravel and scatter plastic strips. If you still want to use a woven fabric, you'll need to cauterize the cut edges with a gas burner to seal them.

Widely spaced plants are best suited for growing through a weed-blocking fabric. Closely spaced crops, such as lettuce, chard, and cabbage, are less suitable. There will be more holes in the fabric letting light in and allowing weeds to flourish. It also won't work to sow seeds under fabric. If any seed germinates, the plant will have a hard time finding a way through the fabric.

Squash and pumpkins are perfect candidates for growing through fabric because they are widely spaced and also cover the surface quickly with their tendrils. The fruit won't get dirty from the soil, which is another advantage. Potatoes can work but you'll need to help the stem and leaves find their way up through the fabric.

CROPS THAT ARE NOT PRE-CULTIVATED

Carrots, parsnips, salsify, parsley root, and scorzonera cannot be pre-cultivated! The root threads will unfailingly break at planting and the root will grow deformed or bifurcated.

Newly planted squash

It is perfectly okay to make holes in the
soil to set out your plants in the beds.

POTTING UP FOR STABILITY AND STRENGTH

• Plants that grow in a small soil volume grow against the pot sides and the roots separate. As the plant grows, it is potted up into a larger pot and will fill the new space with roots. The result is a stable root system that holds the soil volume together. When the plant is lifted out of the pot for transplanting into your garden, the soil is attached and the roots are protected.

• Fruiting plants like artichokes, eggplants, chili peppers, and tomatoes need to develop strong roots before they are planted out in beds. This means as they grow they need to be potted up into larger and larger pots. As a general rule: roots should fill a 2¾ inch to 3 in. (7 cm–8 cm) -diameter pot before it is time to move it into a garden bed.

• Cabbage doesn't really need potting up but it is less likely to be attacked or damaged by insects if potted up and allowed to grow in a pot for about six weeks before going into the garden.

SOWING IN COMPOST SOIL

Sowing and planting in compost soil works great. You can use garden, kitchen, or livestock compost. Still, it's vital to make sure the compost is fully processed and has taken on the characteristics and smell of soil. This applies especially to livestock compost, which has to be fully processed and aged. Keep an eye out for this:

• Any kind of compost not fully processed will contain elements that inhibit germination and can harm plant roots. The new plants risk malnutrition as working microbes steal nutrients from the material.

• Livestock compost that is not fully processed may contain a lot of nitrogen. The risk is that small fragile roots will get burned. (Read more about compost on p. 99–117.)

DIRECT SOWING—STRAIGHT INTO THE GARDEN BED

Most vegetable seeds can be directly sown into the garden bed once the soil/compost is dry and crumbly and warm enough. Take my advice—don't be in too much of a hurry. Seeds that are sown in properly warmed soil result in healthy plants that will grow fast and vigorously.

You can sow directly into a compost bed. In a mulched bed you will need to move the plant matter out of the way. If the plant matter isn't totally decomposed you'll have to add rows of soil or crumbly compost to sow in. Leave the rows open until the seeds have germinated. Once the plants are big enough to not be smothered you can lay mulching material between them.

How to do it:

- Make rows with the edge of your hand or with the back of a rake. Water the row generously before adding seeds.
- Place the seeds in the row. Cover with a layer of soil or compost and tamp down so the seeds have contact all around. No need to water. The dry compost/soil works as a barrier stopping the humidity in the row from evaporating, so the seeds can germinate undisturbed. There is also less risk that you rinse off seeds if you don't have to water. Note what you have sown, and where.
- If you wish, cover the sown rows with floating row cover during the first weeks. Water regularly once the first leaves, the cotyledons, have appeared, and thin out the plants if they are spaced too closely.

Broadcast sowing and diagonal sowing

- Fast-growing vegetables like dill, radishes, arugula, and leaf lettuce can be broadcast (i.e. the seeds are sprinkled out evenly over the growing bed and then covered with soil or compost).
- Diagonal sowing distributes the seeds in a way that produces a square pattern. The seeds are sown with enough space between them to allow the plants to grow to full mature size. Diagonal sowing allows more seeds to be sown, and as a result produces more vegetables than when seeds are sown in straight rows.

Direct sowing—pros and cons

- The advantage of direct sowing is it's fast and you don't have the hassle of indoor seed starting, which is time-consuming and demands extra material and space.
- The disadvantage is that the soil is not used effectively. Seeds occupy space in the garden beds while germinating, and there will be gaps where seeds didn't germinate. The young plants are also much more vulnerable to attacks from diseases and pests than pre-cultivated plants.

It is time to sow!

Different areas within the same geographic region may vary enormously in temperature, which makes it impossible to establish a general time-line for direct sowing. Spring sowing will definitely be much simpler if you measure soil temperature instead of guessing by following the calendar.

Soil temperature determines whether the seeds can germinate successfully:

- 39.2°F–41°F (4°C–5°C)–broad beans, yellow onions
- 41°F–42.8°F (5°C–6°C)–dill, kohlrabi, turnip, parsnip, parsley, arugula, radish, lettuce, spinach, peas
- 46.4°F (8°C)–potatoes
- 50°F (10°C)–kale, chard, carrot, beets
- 53.6°F (12°C)–beans, red onions
- 59°F (15°C)–pumpkin, squash, early varieties of corn

TO THE RESCUE— FLOATING ROW COVERS

- Placing a floating row cover over sown seeds retains warmth and humidity in the soil and keeps the seeds safe from thieving birds. Place the cover on top of the rows and anchor it with stones or pieces of wood.
- Placed over fragile plants, the cover will retain warmth and protect against winds, insects, and pests. Place the cover over hoops or other construction to avoid direct contact with the plants.
- Row covers are great even with mulched beds as it anchors fly-away plant material. It also stops birds from using the mulch as building material in the spring.

FOUR-YEAR CROP ROTATION

1st change—Nourishing plants. Beans, peas, and other legumes take nitrogen from the air and collect nutrition for the soil.

2nd change—Nutritionally demanding plants. This is your cabbage, cucumber, squash, pumpkin, celery, garlic, and leeks. They use up the nutrition the 1st change has collected.

3rd change—Reasonable demand for nutrition. These are the root vegetables, onions, dill, parsley, lettuce, and other greens. Good followers after 2nd change used up a lot of nutrients.

4th change—Least demand for nutrition. Potatoes are very unassuming and manage very well even though 3rd change used up nutrients.

CROP ROTATION

In organic kitchen gardens, the same crop should not be grown in the same place year after year. Different vegetables use the soil in their own ways, and each has their individual nutritional needs. For this reason, whole plant families are moved around in a system where the soil is encouraged to practice self-preservation. Crop rotation lessens the risk for soil-borne diseases, and fortunately, certain pests are confused by the change in location from year to year. The most common rotation in kitchen gardens is over a four-year stretch, while professional growers might use a rotation of up to twelve years. The principle for crop rotation is as follows:

• Certain plants nourish the soil, others demand lots of nutrients, and some are unassuming. Rotation is decided by the nutritional needs of each.

• The same diseases often affect plants in the same families. That's a good reason to grow them together, and to have a break between four to seven years before any of them return to the same garden bed.

• Plants work the soil in various ways. Some have shallow roots that break up the soil surface and others have strong roots that penetrate and loosen the soil deeper down. Some plants also leave a lot of plant matter that can be reused for mulching. With the No-Dig gardening method, the need for crop rotation is not quite as pronounced. This is because a soil that is rich in fungi and mycorrhiza, continually receiving organic plant matter, is strong and healthy. This way there is less risk of an area becoming depleted. By planting mixed beds with many plant varieties, we imitate nature's growing order and the growth cycle looks after itself. It is wise, however, to learn how crop rotation works and to act without hesitation, shifting areas for plant families affected by diseases and

COMMON EXCEPTIONS IN FOUR-YEAR CROP ROTATION

No rules without exceptions, right? Some plants grow best together with plants from other families, some can be sown wherever you feel like it, and then some need a break of seven years before they can place a root in the same soil. Research done on large-scale crop rotation gives these points of reference:

• Cabbage plants and legumes should not return to the same area until after a seven-year break because of the risk of contracting clump root and wilting disease, which deforms roots and plants.

• Beans and peas are not happy neighbors even if they are related. Grow them apart from each other.

• Tomatoes are seldom grown in crop rotation. They are best grown in a sunny, extra warm area in the kitchen garden, in pots or in greenhouses. Change the growing area yearly to protect them from attacks by nasty nematodes. Never grow tomatoes near potatoes. They can fall foul of the same disease, late blight.

• Leeks, in contrast to other onion plants, need plenty of nutrients. It is suitable to grow them together with other nutrient-demanding crops like cabbage, even if they are not related.

• Plant leafy greens and crops like lettuce, radishes, spinach, New Zealand spinach, root vegetables, chard, and corn wherever you find a space. There is always room for new combinations each year when you use a crop rotation schedule as a base. The "free" plants don't seem to end up in exactly the same places anyway. It's wise to make sure they aren't planted too close to last year's space to prevent any overwintering pests finding their way to host plants.

pests. (Read more about this in the chapter Thugs in the garden bed, on p. 194.) It is a pure win-win situation growing legumes in different areas each year because they take nitrogen from the air and bind it in their roots, fertilizing the soil purely by their presence.

It's easier keeping an eye on your crops once you understand crop rotation. So as not to forget, carefully note down where, what, and why something was grown. Then you are free to sow and plan, making it as beautiful as you desire.

Marigolds look good alongside kale, and they have an odor pests dislike.

PLANT FAMILIES—COMMON MEMBERS

Legumes/pulses, *Fabaceae*—peas, beans
Cruciferous plants, *Brassicaceae*—cauliflower, broccoli, kale, white cabbage, turnip, kohlrabi
Cucumber plants, *Curcurbitaceae*—cucumber, squash, pumpkin
Goosefoot plants, *Chenopodiaceae*—chard, spinach, beets
Umbellifers, *Apiaceae*—dill, fennel, carrot, parsley, celeriac
Composites, *Asteraceae*—lettuce, many flowers
Alliaceous plants, *Alliaceae*—onion, garlic
Nightshades, *Solanaceae*—eggplant, bell peppers, tomato, potato

CLIMATE-SMART PERENNIALS

Perennials are herbaceous plants that live several years. They die down to the ground in the winter and start growing again in the spring. Perennials are perfect for No-Dig gardens as they stay where they were planted.

Perennials aren't just easy to grow, they are also very climate smart. Their presence locks carbon in the soil, and the root system retains nutrients in the soil because the roots don't die off during winter. Many perennials flower early, which benefits pollinators, and perennials often produce when nothing else has emerged yet. We usually talk about perennials in reference to decorative and cutting gardens but they have their place in the vegetable beds, too. Many perennials aren't just lovely to look at; they are also delicious to eat. Growing perennial vegetables has many advantages. First of all, they extend the growing season because some of them get going as soon as the frost is out of the ground, and others produce all the way until mid-winter. Perennials are also very wholesome thanks to their deep and permanent root systems that provide excellent access to nutrients and minerals in an undisturbed soil. Their appearance early in the spring lets them benefit from plenty of sunlight, which also increases the nutritional richness. Tough and resistant, many perennial vegetables have retained the wild plant's natural defenses like sour flavors and coarse leaves and, as a result, have good resistance both to diseases and pests.

It's highly rewarding to grow perennials, as they return year after year. You don't have to fuss with yearly seed buying and indoor seed starting. Their well-developed root systems reach moisture deep underground so they seldom need watering once they're established in the garden bed. Perennials might need to be thinned out and separated if they grow too big, or possibly exchanged for new specimens when they show signs

BUSHES ON THE SLOPE

Berry bushes, grapes, and other ligneous (i.e. woody-stemmed) plants can be grown without problems in No-Dig garden beds. The plants establish themselves very well in the raised, humus-rich and warm soils that mulched and composted beds offer. Don't forget to calculate the spread of the growing plants—many bushes like to hog space.

of diminishing growth. Otherwise, their care is mostly springtime weeding and application of cover, like compost or organic plant matter, during the growing season and before winter arrives.

We don't plant perennial vegetables to replace the annuals—we do it as a complement. To have both perennials and annuals in the No-Dig kitchen garden ensures both reliable crops and crops that might not have been at the forefront earlier, but are now an exciting and climate-smart addition to the menu. (Get tips on good perennials to grow on p. 179–185.)

Growing perennials—things to keep in mind

Raised beds. Grow perennials in raised beds according to the lasagna and compost bed principles. A raised bed equals warmth and good drainage. The humidity is retained with organic plant matter covers.

Micro-climate. Plant perennials in a warm, protected area. This will provide them with good growing conditions and facilitate their overwintering. House walls and stonewalls collect warmth; tall windbreaks protect against strong winds; a pergola can support wintergreen growth to make a dense and protective wall.

Fertilizer boosts. Perennials seldom need additional boosts of fertilizer above what they get from compost and organic mulch. That said, during their most intense production/harvest period it doesn't hurt to add some grass clippings or a dose of liquid fertilizer. (Read more about this in the chapter on nutrition on p. 118.)

Soil cover. Layer additional compost and/or organic plant mulch each fall to insulate plant roots for the winter. This also provides material for the microorganisms in the ground to work with. The compost doesn't need to be completely decomposed. Wood chips and tree bark usually work well.

Drainage. The garden bed needs good drainage as sensitive roots don't like wet feet.

CARE

Your plantings need regular attention and care. A daily walk-around is likely necessary to keep an eye on things. The care will be easier if you do a bit here and there each day.

Water. All plants need continual access to water, both because of thirst and also to dissolve nutrients, making them available to the plant roots. With compost beds, this is not a problem. The soil is never bare and the moisture doesn't evaporate. The beds also have a large amount of moisture-trapping humus, the pores of which move oxygen and water around freely. It is a plus when the soil is undisturbed, giving the plants access to moisture deep in the ground. In other words, mulched or compost covered beds need only infrequent watering.

There are, of course, some exceptions. It is important to water when sowing and planting the garden beds. This provides the seeds and plants with the conditions to start off on the right foot. You'll also need to check moisture levels during the first few weeks, making sure the plants are doing well. Some crops, like fast-growing lettuce and plants with shallow roots, need lots of moisture and may need some extra water. Fruiting plants want plenty of water when they flower and set fruit; it makes it easier for swelling seedpods, cobs, and fruits to develop. Extra water is of course needed during drought conditions.

The mantra when watering is: "A lot, but not often." Better to drench the plants each time than to sprinkle often on the surface. With water deep below the soil surface the plant roots can search downwards and get nutrients, too. Water the soil and roots where it is needed, never on the plants or the leaves themselves. Mildew can start if the plants are close together and the moisture and humidity stays on them. 5¼ gallons–8 gallons (20–30 l) per 10¾ sq. ft. (1 sq. meter) will go to a depth of at least 4 inches (10 cm). Surface watering evaporates quickly and also gives weed seeds moisture to germinate.

DRIP IRRIGATION IN DROUGHT CONDITIONS

The cover material combined with rainfall is usually enough to ensure sufficient humidity for organically mulched beds. They do need help during hot summers, which is awkward when compost or mulch is in the way. One solution is to use a drip irrigation hose, which is placed in the bed before the compost or mulch is added. With a drip hose, the water will seep out slowly and disperse evenly across the garden bed. It is calculated that a drip irrigation hose will save about 70 percent water compared to traditional hose watering methods.

STEP LIGHTLY

Never trample in the garden beds. Each step compresses vital oxygen and water paths, making life difficult for the soil organisms. If the beds are too large, and you can't reach from each side, put down planks for walking on. This spreads out the pressure and saves the soil texture.

WEEDS ARE NATURE'S BAND-AID

Bare soil needs to be covered as soon as possible. If left bare, the soil can be washed away and the microorganisms will be harmed. Pioneer species quickly grow to cover bare soil, which is Nature's way of putting a bandage on the damage. A covered, undisturbed soil doesn't call for help, which means that weeds need to really use force to make an appearance.

Use a watering can without a sprinkler head, a hose, an irrigation hose, or some other kind of drip set-up underneath the cover. Well-established perennials and bushes don't need frequent watering, except during prolonged droughts.

Thin out. Crops that grow too closely need to be thinned out to let the remaining vegetables grow to full size. Imagine the size of a mature vegetable and thin accordingly. When you cluster sow, the vegetables more or less climb all over each other, but you still need to thin out within the clusters. Thinned-out delicate plants can be used in cooking. Immature carrot tops and beet greens are great in salads. (Read more about cluster sowing on p. 75.)

Hill/cover with soil. Vegetables such as potatoes, leeks, and sometimes carrots, need to be hilled for stability and protection against sunlight. Push soil, compost, or more organic mulch material up against the plant. It is vital to hill potatoes as they will turn green and toxic if they are exposed to sunlight. Potatoes may also yield a bigger harvest if shallow roots get an extra layer of organic plant matter.

Weed and watch. Weeding is a very small chapter in No-Dig and mulched gardening. There just isn't enough space for weeds to get established. If you did go after the weeds thoroughly in the spring, there will be minimal weeding during the summer; what weeds appear will be easily raked or pulled out as they poke up.

To give the plants time to establish themselves, you do need to keep an eye out for weeds and diligently remove them after sowing and planting. During the rest of the season you mostly need to regularly check on the beds and keep an eye out for slugs and other unwelcome visitors. (Read more in the chapter Thugs in the garden bed on p. 194.)

Fill in and harvest. Your inspection tours provide a good way to discover and cover the gaps where seeds and plants didn't make it. Sow seeds or fill in with pre-cultivated plants. Also continue to replenish the mulched beds with organic plant matter. Harvest as things mature and succession sow new seeds and plants whenever there is a gap in a bed.

Fertilize. Fertilizing has low priority in the No-Dig garden beds, as the organisms in the undisturbed soil, by themselves, create a natural nutritional network from which plant roots can get energy. It's calculated it takes three years from the beginning for a No-Dig garden bed, if it has been provided regularly with organic mulch and/or compost, to be nutritionally self-sufficient. Beds that are used for intensive cultivation, however, may need an extra dose of fertilizer. Only some liquid fertilizer would be required because a properly cared for mulch or compost bed is very rich in humus.

The garden beds might need a bit of a helping hand before they are established, especially as a lot of nitrogen is needed to get vegetative growth started. Fully processed livestock manure, biochar, and bokashi compost are perfect for both mulch and compost beds. Liquid fertilizers like gold water (urine), nettle water, comfrey water, manure water, or commercial organic fertilizer are also good to use. (Read more in the chapter about nutrition, p. 118.)

FERTILIZING BASICS

It is hard to tell exactly when specific vegetables need to be given an all-purpose and short-term fertilizing boost; you'll need to observe and judge by plant health. There are a few basics, though, to follow:

• Fertilize when you plant and then repeat lightly over the following three (3) years. After this, it is enough to cover the soil and give it a few rations of liquid nutrition in the spring.

• Fertilize little but often. Too much fertilizer damages both plants and the environment. The plants develop less flavor and won't keep, while excess fertilizer leaks out and causes eutrophication of natural water sources.

• In early summer, when growth is at its strongest, demanding plants like pumpkin, squash, cucumber, cabbage, tomatoes, and leeks want a boost of liquid fertilizer with nitrogen or a 4-inch (10-cm) layer of grass clippings.

• Plants that are not growing well need an addition of grass cuttings or nitrogen-rich fertilizer to get going again.

• Never add a short-term boost in the fall. The plants won't have time to absorb the nutrition and fertilizer will leak and cause eutrophication of natural water sources.

Garden beds—specific care

Compost, mulch, and hügel beds all follow the same cultivation principle. What separates them is how the cover material is handled before, during, and after the growing season.

Care of composted beds

Fall preparation. Place a 2-inch (5-cm) layer of new compost on the bed once the season is past—that way you are prepared for next year. Cover with a floating row cover, straw, or grass that lets through moisture while minimizing leakage of carbon dioxide, smothers runner-spread weeds, and prevents seeded weeds from getting a foothold. Replenishing in the fall gives the compost time to settle and become soft and nice for spring sowing and planting. You can also add compost before planting in the spring. Make sure it is thoroughly processed.

Warm the soil in spring. Remove the organic cover matter or floating row cover a few weeks before sowing or planting to allow the sunshine to warm up the bed.

Finishing touches and weeding. Break up any clods with a rake. Pull and remove any weeds just before sowing or planting. Pull runner-spread weeds and push away seed weeds with a garden hoe.

Care of mulched beds

Fall preparation. Add both nitrogen and carbon-rich winter mulch. Microorganisms are active even in the frozen ground, working on the mulch during winter. The cover also retains the warmth, which allows worms to continue working the soil. Use all the material you can get your hands on. It's preferable to use a bit thicker layers of airy material, thinner layers of grass cuttings, and other materials which otherwise risk getting compacted.

Warm the soil in spring. The leftover cover works as insulation and retains the winter cold in the spring. Prepare for spring sowing and planting by pushing aside the cover material, rake in a few planting rows, and let the sun warm the soil a few weeks before it is time to sow and plant. Remember, it's more practical to have the cover material already placed on the bed before sowing and planting. You'll risk smothering seeds and fragile plants if you add organic mulch afterwards.

Finishing touches and weeding. Break up any clods with a rake. Interrupt and remove any weeds just before sowing and planting. Pull up runner-spread weeds and remove seed weeds with a hoe.

Cover continually. The cover layer on a mulched bed should always be 6–7 inches (15 cm–20 cm) thick, so keep adding to it as the mulch decomposes.

Place organic plant matter between the rows of small plants and a little more densely around larger plants. Never place mulch up against the plant stems or leaves as it might make them rot. Use all the mulching material you have. Layer carbon-rich with nitrogen-rich so the decomposing process doesn't steal nutrition from the plants. Grass clippings are the easiest to get your hands on during the summer; but only use it, at most, three times per season in 4-inch (10-cm) layers. If you use more, mix the clippings with old leaves, some straw, or other carbon-rich materials to balance the nitrogen content. Try to lay mulch ridges a bit thicker between the vegetable rows—it is easy to push in between the plants once it's decomposed.

Special section:

Care of hügel beds

The hügel bed requires a bit more attentive care due to its special properties, but it also rewards you plenty. This special garden bed can be sown and planted following the same principle as mulch and compost beds. Weed, put in finishing touches in the fall, and warm the soil in spring following your growing agenda.

However, remember:

Water. A hügel bed accumulates water in the bottom timber and retains moisture well. But the surface may dry out before the breakdown of materials starts in earnest, so you need to check if water is needed.

Fertilizer boost. Enough nutrients should be created during the breakdown of the building materials inside the bed. However, a lot of nitrogen is used to break down carbon-rich matter, so add plenty of mulch and/or compost and some liquid fertilizer if the plants are lagging behind in growth. (See the chapter on nutrition, p. 118.)

START OUT WITH SHALLOW-ROOTED PLANTS

Before decomposition of the logs has started in earnest, the planting depth in a hügel bed is not very generous. Start out with shallow-rooted plants. Wait to transplant or seed deeper-rooted plants until some of the material in the bed has broken down.

MAXIMIZED HARVESTS

No-Dig beds that are continually fed lots of organic matter become humus-rich and very nutritious. You can have both a long season and large yields if you use the beds cleverly. Of course, you may be perfectly happy with just one harvest per season; and the bed, like the yield, can still be large. If you're interested, there are still a lot of tips and tricks to help you profit to the fullest extent from strong and healthy soil in your No-Dig garden beds.

Plant spacing

A well-functioning No-Dig bed has good access to nutrition, which means that plants can stand close together. You can even sometimes ignore the seed packet instructions for row and plant spacing. Instead, imagine the size of the full-grown plant and then sow or plant so the plants can grow without having to jostle for space.

It is difficult to give exact measurements, but a guideline is that you want the upper part of the plants to have enough space so they don't bump into each other. The plants manage on their own down in the soil where there is lots of space for roots. In general, close planting gives the crop a favorable microclimate, which also retains humidity and allows for less watering than a vegetable bed where plants are widely spaced.

A few pointers:

- Onions, leeks, and garlic can grow much closer together than the instructions usually specify.
- Root vegetables can be sown or planted with the final desired harvest size in mind.
- Lettuce and other leafy greens that are harvested from the outside in can be spaced with 7 in. (20 cm) between them.
- Fruiting plants like tomatoes, beans, and squash need plenty of space. Follow the seed packet instructions for plant spacing.

Staggered planting

It's easy to grow produce efficiently with a nursery for growing/forcing plants, either indoors or in a protected corner of the garden. While the plants grow in pots, planting cells, and boxes for a week up to a few months, other things can grow in the beds. After these are harvested, the new pre-cultivated plants are set out. They are now so big it won't take long for them to be harvest ready. To profit from large and continual harvests, it is smart to force even fast-growing crops (i.e. plants with shorter development time) that are usually sown directly into the garden beds.

When forcing plants in trays and cells, it's easy to water and keep an eye on what is actually growing. You can also fill any gaps in the vegetable garden if forced plants are at hand. Forced plants are also sturdier and in good condition to resist diseases and pests. By continually forcing plants you'll have an extended season and the opportunity to harvest several times per season in the same area. It is great to be able to harvest young, fresh produce, even in late summer.

Some tips:

- Most plants can be successfully sown in pots or planting cells. Beets in a variety of colors, chard, radishes, turnips, and kohlrabi grow well in planting cells and thrive once planted in the beds.
- Squash and pumpkins demand individual pots. They want to be planted at the same depth as they were in the pot.
- Broad beans, bush beans, and sugar peas are great to have on hand. Beans have fragile roots and should be forced singly in large paper or peat pots. The entire pot should be planted directly in the soil to keep the roots from being damaged. Beans also like to stay at the same level as they were in the pot.
Broadcast/wide sowing in sowing boxes is simple and a time saver. It's very suitable for small seeds and seeds that germinate a bit haphazardly like cabbage, basil, lettuce, as well as parsley, coriander, and dill. Cover the bottom of a sowing box with soil. Water and then sprinkle seeds over the surface. Cover with soil and water carefully so it is neither too dry nor too wet. Separate and transplant the seedlings once they appear. Don't leave them to grow crowded for too long. Plant green herbs in compact tufts.
- Transplanting. Lettuce, cabbage, and different kinds of onions that are sown together in trays and sowing boxes benefit

from being transplanted when very young (i.e. separated and potted up) once the growing space is getting crowded. They can be transplanted together, but into larger trays with holes for bottom drainage. Fill the tray with potting soil or compost and make holes for the plants with a dibber. Space the plants about one inch apart. Pry the plants carefully out of the sowing box with the dibber and move them to the larger tray. Place the plants slightly deeper in this larger tray so they grow sturdy. These plants can spend quite a long time in this larger tray but will need a ration of liquid fertilizer once a week. (See chapter on nutrition on p. 118.) Watering, care, and handling is simpler with all the plants in the same tray, as opposed to being grown in individual pots.

- Forced greens and many root vegetables develop nicely if placed out in the vegetable beds even when young, so they don't need to be potted up. This way the roots are minimally disturbed and you'll save time and space in the nursery. Plants like lettuce and beets can be successfully handled like this, as long as they have five true leaves when they are planted out.

Note that carrots, parsnips, salsify, parsley root, and scorzonera cannot be pre-cultivated/forced and transplanted.

Companion planting and interplanting

Companion planting and interplanting between rows is a way to maximize yield from the same growing area, saving you both time and space. Companion planting contributes to a healthy soil because different plants use and work the soil in different ways. Companion planting can also protect against insects and pests searching for a specific kind of plant. Pests flee the garden bed when their prey is planted alongside something they dislike.

If plants are growing too close together, they might compete with each other and therefore become stunted as they grow, which isn't good. The solution is to resist the temptation to leave the vegetables growing for too long. Instead, harvest what is ready and leave the space for the other plants to spread out.

Some examples:

- Grow fast-growing crops like radish, lettuce, dill, and coriander together with slower-growing cabbages like broccoli, Brussels sprouts, and kale. When the bed is crowded, harvest the fast-growing vegetables/herbs to open up the space for the slow-growing vegetables to spread out.
- Grow plants that develop above ground together with below ground vegetables. For example: lettuce with root vegetables, or parsley and dill together with onions. The crops utilize the soil at different levels, which allows them to grow together efficiently.
- Mâche lettuce, sometimes called winter lettuce or field lettuce, grows well in the shade from larger plants. Once the larger plants are harvested or have died down for the winter, mâche comes into its own.
- Combine tall plants with shorter ones that spread in between and under the plants. For example: lettuce or low string beans below leeks or corn; or New Zealand spinach underneath tomatoes.
- Plant flowers in the vegetable beds. Marigolds put nematodes (roundworms, earth parasites) on the run. They also attract humble/bumble bees, honey bees, and other beneficial insects that help pollinate the vegetables.

Cluster planting

Sow seeds in clusters instead of one by one in a row and you'll get more vegetables from the same surface. Sow in groups of three (3) to six (6) seeds, either directly into the garden bed or in pots and trays for transplanting out later. Vegetables that grow in clusters jostle for space and, as a result, grow to different sizes. Choose to either harvest the whole cluster or just the largest vegetables, letting the smaller grow some more. Suitable vegetables to grow in clusters are onions, chives, leeks, parsnips, radishes, and dill. Beets are also excellent for growing in clusters as each seed has the germs for several plants. By not thinning the small plants, but letting them grow, you'll end up with great clusters of beets to harvest. Even broad beans can be grown this way; the mature plants can be tied together to support each other.

Combine low-growing plants with tall ones to maximize the growing surface. Here mung beans and lentils are grown as cover crop fertilizer under cabbage.

Sow fewer but frequently

When you sow many seeds of the same variety all at once, you'll end up eating the same thing too many days in a row. Sow fewer seeds at a time and your harvest will be spread out, and your menu more interesting. For example: every other week sow four or five seeds each of five different kinds of lettuce to have different flavors and colors.

Succession planting for multiple harvests

Once the early vegetables are harvested, sow new seeds where there are gaps in the garden beds. That way the soil is never bare and you'll extend the growing season at the same time. Summer sown crops demand more frequent watering than the crops sown in spring. Check often on the newly sown areas.

- Grow fast-growing leafy greens like lettuce, spinach, and arugula early in the season. Plant or seed slower-growing crops like beets, cabbage, and potatoes when you have harvested the fast-growing ones. Early in fall, when the slower crops have been harvested, fill the gaps with new fast-growing plants such as leaf lettuce, mâche, chives, Asian greens, and spinach, which will mature within a month and are hardy enough for a drop in temperature.
- Leafy greens, bush beans, fennel, radishes, lettuce, summer carrots, daikon radish, turnip, and chard can be sown in succession throughout the summer. Choose varieties that are described as fast-growing or early maturing.
- Bok choy, Welsh/salad onions, sugar peas, mâche lettuce, dill, radishes, and arugula can also be sown in July.
- Direct sow peas in July and you have a harvest around September.
- Set out pre-cultivated/forced broccoli and kale plants once the potatoes are done. Kale can handle some frost and can be harvested during fall.
- Examples of forced plants that are good to have on hand are: lettuce, Bok choy, leafy cabbage, broccoli, fennel, spinach, New Zealand spinach, turnip, and Pak choi.
- Forced potato plants are perfect to plant out once onions are harvested.

VEGETABLES THAT CAN WEATHER A FROSTY NIGHT

Kale
Tuscan cabbage/kale
Jerusalem artichoke
Kohlrabi
Mâche lettuce
Carrot
Parsnip
Leek
Celeriac

Long-lived greens—leaf by leaf

Using a bit of planning you can give your lettuce, spinach, and chard an extended fruitful life. Sow the seeds with 7 in. (20 cm) between them, slightly closer for spinach and chard, and the plants will have enough space, nutrients, and humidity to keep producing leaves over a long period. Pick a few leaves each time from each plant, working from the outside in. The plant grows new from the center, so you can keep picking the outer leaves over and over from the same plant.

Lettuce that starts to bolt becomes bitter, so harvest the complete plant once it is shaping into a pyramid. If you like a slightly tart flavor, the tiny leaves on flowering lettuce are for you. The sweet, if a bit tart, stem is also nice grilled or roasted.

Leafy greens that regrow after harvest

Many leafy greens will regenerate even after the whole plant has been harvested. Leave ¾ in. to 1¼ in. (2 cm–3 cm) of the plant when you cut it off and it will grow new leaves. You don't need any extra nutrition if you put grass clippings between the plants; otherwise you may have to give a short-term boost with liquid fertilizer a few times during the season.

A few sure-fire cut and come again vegetables are dill, leaf lettuce, parsley, purslane, kale, New Zealand spinach, Tuscan kale/cabbage, mâche lettuce, and mizuna (Japanese) cabbage.

Fall and winter growing

Some seeds can be sown in the fall for a harvest in the winter or for vegetables in the spring.

- Mâche, also called winter lettuce or field lettuce, can be sown in late August for a fall harvest. If sown later, it can be harvested in the winter and early spring. Mâche lettuce can take both freezing temperatures and thawing. It can be harvested even if it is covered by snow.

- Spinach can be sown in August and at the beginning of September. Cover with straw to overwinter and harvest in late spring.
- Dill, carrots, and parsley, normally sown in early spring, can be sown in the fall as well.

  The seeds rest in the soil during the winter, waiting for the warmth, germinating when the soil is warm enough. This results in an early harvest and less work in the spring, as the early sowing is already done. Sow the seeds just before the ground freezes because, if they start growing in the fall, the plants will not survive the cold.

Harvest at the right time

Once the crops are ready to harvest the big feast starts. There are plenty of fresh vegetables to both eat and save, and space is liberated in the garden beds for sowing and planting new crops. Harvesting correctly is an important part of gardening because many plants produce more abundantly the more frequently they're harvested. By visiting the kitchen garden often you can keep an eye on and remove damaged or rotting plant matter that would attract slugs and other pests. You also notice if the plants need water or protection.

It is best to bring two baskets or buckets at harvest time; one for the vegetables and one for tops, damaged leaves, weeds, and other garden debris to be composted or used as mulching material. Use a knife for crops that are not picked by hand. Tugging risks damaging the plants. Check thoroughly among the plants so you don't overlook any hidden vegetables.

TIPS FOR LETTUCE AND SPINACH

• Lettuce won't germinate if the soil temperature is above 68°F (20°C), so it is no use sowing lettuce in the height of summer. There is a way around this though—water the soil with ice water before sowing. This gives the seeds a chance to germinate, even in the summer heat. Another way is by broadcasting seeds in a tray with soil that has been watered with ice-cold water. Place the sown seed tray in a cool place, in the shade or in a refrigerator, until the seeds have germinated and the first leaves have appeared. Transplant them into the vegetable bed.

• Spinach needs to rest during the night and has a tendency to bolt if days are too long or hot. Sow spinach early in the spring, taking a break in July, and restart the sowing in August to avoid the bolting problem.

EASY-TO-GROW VEGETABLES

Chard, yellow and red onion, carrots, leaf lettuce, potatoes, arugula, and radishes are all very easy to grow.

Something to keep in mind:

- Harvest regularly when the vegetables are ready. If not harvested when ready, some vegetables will bolt and set seed, which means that the plant believes its work is now done. Others grow to enormous size and become woody and bland in flavor. Enjoy your harvest by eating it fresh, freezing it, or putting it up.
- Harvest to encourage new growth. Squash, peas, and beans are plants that continue to produce the more they are harvested. Dill, parsley, coriander, spinach, and many other leafy greens will re-grow if you cut them down to ¾ in.–1¼ in. (2 cm–3 cm) height.
- Harvest potatoes with a pitchfork, hand fork, or with your hand to minimize the risk of tool damage to the potatoes. If you're impatient for an early harvest, pick the potatoes one by one from the soil, but leave the plant be so it can develop more potatoes. Always take care to collect even the smallest potatoes. If they are left in the soil they can start growing and disturb what is meant to grow there the next season.

Make space for new crops

It's fast and easy to clean up a No-Dig bed after a harvest to make room for new seeds and plants. You'll just need to remove garden debris like lettuce, cabbage, and spinach stems, and then even out the surface. Always leave the roots in the soil. If the legumes are cut off just below the soil surface some nitrogen-binding nodules might still be there to the benefit of future crops.

Messy bed = humus-rich soil

When the last harvest is over, and it is time to prepare the beds for winter, it's really quite silly to make things too neat and proper-looking. Cut down plant debris and add it to the compost pile or use it to mulch the beds. Leave the roots in the ground. They add humus elements and nutrients when they decompose, and they leave behind tunnels for oxygen and water. A great deal of the humus in fine soil is the result of leftover plant roots combined with strong fungal systems.

Old plant debris left on the garden bed might look messy but it is rich humus in the making.

Growing frames and greenhouses

Growing frames, greenhouses, and growing tunnels provide both earlier and longer growing seasons and are good compliments to garden beds.

A growing frame is a bottomless box with a see-through lid. It is used as a smaller alternative to a greenhouse and works for pre-cultivating, growing, hardening-off, and overwintering. There are two versions of growing frames: heated and cold frames. The temperature in the heated frame is elevated by the help of heat-producing livestock manure. Using this, it's possible to grow outdoors during late winter. Cold frames are heated by the sun and keep the soil evenly warm as long as there is light and temperatures are not too cold.

Greenhouses and growing tunnels extend the growing season and make life more comfortable for fragile plants. Just like frames, greenhouses come heated or unheated. The heated greenhouse has a heat source that keeps the greenhouse at 59°F (15°C) year round, making it possible to grow throughout the year and also to overwinter plants. An unheated greenhouse is warmed by the sun and is used to increase the temperature for heat-loving plants during the warmer part of the year.

There's a whole science around the building of frames and choosing a greenhouse. There are many good books on the subject and you can find a lot of information online. Just remember: not even in a growing frame, greenhouse, or growing tunnel is there a need for digging. Just prepare your No-Dig planting as explained.

COVER/MULCHING
MATERIALS & COMPOST

The basic principle is the same whether you use compost or non-decomposed mulching material in your No-Dig garden beds: organic plant matter provides organisms with something to turn into nutrition and humus.

The materials act a bit differently depending on their origin and shape, just as where and when they are placed on the beds. Learning how different kinds of mulch and compost react goes a long way toward understanding what happens in the garden beds and why.

COVER/MULCHING MATERIAL FOR HUMUS AND NUTRITION

When you cover a garden bed with a layer of organic plant matter it's like creating compost directly on the growth surface. That's why it's often called direct composting, or surface composting. The difference with processed compost is it doesn't have to pass through the compost bin. Instead, the microorganisms get lots of material to break down directly in the bed.

Basically, any kind of organic material can be used to mulch beds. As the grower, you will develop a sure eye for what works and when. Fresh material contains plenty of nutrition. Dry material gives the soil structure, but with less nutrition. By learning the different properties of the materials you can pair the nutritional needs of the soil and plants or balance a possible excess.

Many gardens produce enough organic materials to provide ample amounts of food for the soil, which is an environmental advantage as nothing needs to be burned or driven to recycling facilities. However, sometimes additional materials might be required from outside. Everything from a neighbor's grass clippings, the riding school's manure pile, or old straw and damaged silage bales is a gold mine for mulched garden beds. The materials are often given free of charge. Transporting them home is often the extent of your expenditure.

It is impossible to say how much nutrition is added through mulching. All soils have their own unique qualities and the organic matter has different origins and properties. However, it is obvious that a balanced feed of different mulching materials provides food for the insects and microorganisms in the soil and a great opportunity to create a healthy environment for your plants.

Mulch materials—varieties, properties, and use

FRESH GRASS CUTTINGS contain all the nutrients plants need. They are especially abundant in nitrogen, which benefits vegetative growth. The nourishment is available to the plants after just a week. Grass cuttings also benefit soil bacteria. A luscious lawn contains more nitrogen than a malnourished and dry one. Even a lawn needs to be fed in order to make nice grass cuttings. Just leave the clippings where they fall a few times per season and the lawn feeds itself. If you don't have enough grass cuttings of your own, ask neighbors and friends. It might also be possible to get grass clippings from cemeteries, parks, or schools. Just make sure that you don't end up with a lot of cigarette butts and plastic debris.
Usage: Two to three times per season, place a 4 in. (10 cm) layer of fresh grass clippings on the garden bed. Legumes, potatoes, root vegetables, and berry bushes should only be covered once per season. Too much affects the structure and is detrimental to the flavor. There might be germinating weed seeds in the clippings but the majority are killed off if the grass layer is thick. Overwintering plants that need a rest period at summer's end should not get a nitrogen boost too late in the season.
Pros: Nitrogen-rich and fast acting. Leaves nutrition for the next year. Feeds the soil with humus elements. Smothers weeds. Retains moisture. Easy to place. Free of charge.

Cons: Might contain grass and weed seeds. Clumps together if it is stored in a pile before being spread out. Attracts slugs and other pests. Is in the way when you want to sow seeds.

HARVEST DEBRIS like plant stalks, rhubarb leaves, bean plants and leafy tops are good mulching materials. Fresh plant matter is nitrogen-rich, which benefits vegetative growth.
Usage: Placed in succession as plant matter becomes available. Plants affected by diseases should not be used.
Pros: Nitrogen-rich. Feeds the soil with humus elements. Smothers weeds. Retains moisture. Easy to place. Free of charge.
Cons: Attracts slugs and other pests.

WEEDS and GARDEN DEBRIS from garden beds, perennial beds, and edge clippings give nutrition and humus. There is less risk for weeds germinating or rooting if they haven't gone to seed and are allowed to dry out before being placed on the bed. Refrain from using noxious runner-spread weeds like ground elder and bindweed as they risk taking root.
Usage: Place in thin layers on the garden bed, preferably on top of some other mulch material where it's allowed to dry out. Cover with other organic material. If weeds start to grow, disturb the roots by raking around in the bed. It's usually simple to pull out any runner-spread weed in a porous bed.
Pros: Nutrient-rich. Feeds the soil with humus elements. Retains moisture. Easy to place. Free of charge.
Cons: Might contain seeds that will germinate and roots that will take hold.

PRESERVE THE GRASS

Grass cuttings can be preserved so they retain all nutrients, and then saved until spring when they can be spread on hungry garden beds. Fill a black garbage bag half full with freshly cut grass clippings. Press out as much air as possible and then knot the bag together securely. Tape over any holes so no oxygen is allowed in the bag. Put the bag aside over winter. Then, in the spring, bring out the bag of fine nutrient-rich grass. Preserved grass clippings ¾ in. (2 cm) thick is the equivalent of 4 in. (10 cm) fresh grass clippings.

DON'T USE MOSS

Don't use moss as mulching material. It is difficult to break down and, if it takes hold in the beds, it might be troublesome to get rid of.

GROW CLOVER IN BETWEEN THE BEDS

Grow an annual subterranean clover in the spaces between the gardening beds to get a good walk path between the rows and some extra mulch. Subclover, *Trifolium subterraneum*, crawls along, is low-growing with a sturdy root system, and helps to bind nitrogen. Sow clover once the kitchen garden plants are established and growing well. Cut down the clover in the paths before it flowers and use the material as mulch.

SEAWEED contains lots of nitrogen and phosphorus. It can be compared to poultry and cow manure. Seaweed is harvested along beaches, preferably near the waterline where it's cleanest. Seaweed can store heavy metals and other toxins; however, bladderwrack seems to absorb less cadmium than other varieties. It is less suitable to collect seaweed along the Baltic Sea beaches due to eutrophication. In some places it is forbidden to pick growing seaweed, so only that which has drifted on to the shoreline can be taken. It's a good idea to ask permission from the landowner if you wish to collect a substantial amount.

Usage: First, rinse the seaweed in freshwater to extract the salt. Then place the seaweed in 2–4 in. (5 cm–10 cm) layers on the garden beds a few times per season. Overwintering plants need to enter a rest period in late summer and shouldn't have late nitrogen rations, so don't mulch too late in the season.

Pros: Provides nutrition and humus elements. Smothers weeds. Retains moisture. Free of charge.

Cons: Time consuming to collect. Might contain heavy metals and other toxins.

STRAW is what is left after cereal grains are extracted from the plants. The remaining stalks and leaves are dried and used as bedding in stables and animal cages. Straw provides an efficient cover and provides lots of humus, but it steals nitrogen from the soil while breaking down. Straw doesn't bring any appreciable nutrition. Feed stores sell straw in small bales. Sometimes farms will give away damaged straw for free.

Usage: Place 2–4 in. (5 cm–10 cm) layers on the beds. It's better to let it decompose some before using so it won't steal quite as much nitrogen and can provide good manure value. Besides, it won't fly away if there is a high wind. Straw works well as winter

Seaweed mulch gives nutrition, protection, and humus.

Straw in different stages of decomposition

cover, but it is good to place some fresh garden debris and some livestock manure underneath to fend off nitrogen loss. Straw is perfect as a path cover between the beds. It can be raked up into the beds once it is broken down.

Pros: Efficient and usually cheap. Feeds the soil humus elements. Smothers weeds. Retains moisture.
Cons: Steals nitrogen when decomposing. Retains the cold in the soil in spring. Attracts slugs and other pests.

HAY is dried forage crop (i.e. a variety of grasses), herbs, and legumes, which are grown as animal fodder. Hay covers efficiently but is rich in carbon and steals nitrogen from the soil during breakdown. It is sold in sacks or bales in feed stores. It is sometimes possible to pick up damaged hay for free at farms.

Usage: It is placed successively in 2–4 in. (5 cm–10 cm) layers on the beds as the mulch layer decomposes.
Pros: Quite nutrient-rich. Covers well. Feeds the soil humus elements. Smothers weeds. Retains moisture.
Cons: Can contain seeds that will germinate. Steals nitrogen while breaking down. Retains the cold in the soil in spring. Attracts slugs and other pests.

SILAGE and **HAY SILAGE** are fresh forage crops (i.e. grasses), herbs, and legumes that have been fermented to preserve nutrients and quality, and then used as animal fodder. The material is fermented in plastic bales in an oxygen-free atmosphere. If a bale breaks it will be unusable as animal fodder but is still excellent as mulching material. It can often be had for free at farms. The bales are heavy, from 772 lb. (350 kg) and upwards. A trailer is needed to transport them. The difference between silage and hay silage is that hay silage is drier.

FRESH AND DRY MULCHING MATERIAL— A BALANCING ART

• Fresh materials like grass cuttings, fresh garden debris, clover, herbs, weeds, and seaweed are often called green material. Green material is very nutritious. The green material adds nitrogen, which benefits vegetative growth. Excess nitrogen causes plants to become overgrown and flabby and fruiting is inhibited. Excess nitrogen is balanced with additional carbon-rich (i.e. dry) material.

• Dry, carbon-rich materials like straw, hay, leaves, bark, and wood chips are often called brown or yellow material. This material is nutritionally poor but adds lots of humus elements. During the first season, nearly no nutrition is released at all. There might even be a temporary lack of nutrients as the materials steal nutrition from the soil while breaking down. The lack of nutrients is balanced out by adding more nitrogen-rich materials, or by watering the mulch with a ration of nitrogen-rich nettle water.

PESTICIDE WARNING!
Pesticides containing aminopyralid and clopyralid are often sprayed on arable land to inhibit or kill weeds. In the United States, these products are only used under strict restrictions concerning succeeding crops because aminopyralid and clopyralid take a long time to break down and can be harmful. Aminopyralid poses the biggest risk.

The problem for hobby growers is that aminopyralid and clopyralid can arrive in the beds through mulching straw or livestock manure if they are sprayed with these pesticides. The result will be deformed and stunted plants in the kitchen garden.

In some countries, farmers who use aminopyralid are not allowed to donate treated straw or manure from the farm. The materials can only be used on their own farm or sold to an energy recovery facility. To be on the safe side, make sure you know what treatments the straw you are using has had in order to avoid all crop failure.

If you suspect that a bed or compost might contain traces of aminopyralid, try out a few pea or bean plants. If the plants grow twisted and the leaves are deformed the bed should not be used for two years. The danger is non-existent if the plants grow normally.

Usage: Silage and hay silage is placed in 4 in. (10 cm) layers successively as the mulch decomposes. It's good to let the material start to decompose before adding it as the process is then well on its way. Place the bale in a cinnamon roll shape to allow falling rain to start the breakdown process. You must use a respirator mask if white mold appears. The mold is not harmful for plant growth but it can cause problems for the grower. An alternative is to spray the bale with water, leaving the material to disintegrate further. It then becomes harmless to the grower.
Pros: Nutrient-rich. Provides humus elements. Smothers weeds. Retains moisture.
Cons: Might contain seeds that will germinate. Retains the cold in the ground in spring. Attracts slugs and other pests.

LEAVES cover well and are a slow-acting soil amendment. Leaves are carbon-rich and use nitrogen during the breakdown process, so you might need to add some extra nitrogen material for balance.
Usage: Finely shred the leaves with the lawn mower before placing them on the garden beds. Whole leaves have a tendency to form large sheets, which will not let oxygen or water through. Place the leaves in 2–4 in. (5 cm–10 cm) layers with even intervals, preferably in the fall as winter cover. Placing planks or other heavy coverings on top will keep the leaves from being blown away.
Pros: Provide excellent humus and fine structure. Smother weeds. Retain moisture. Free of charge.
Cons: Nutritionally poor. Retain the cold in the soil in spring. Might collect into compacted sheets. Heavy to work with when wet. Attract slugs and other pests.

WOOD CHIPS, SHAVINGS, and BARK cover very well and produce good humus levels. The cellulose contributes to the rich fungal life in the soil. The chips, shavings, and bark also contribute to good pH levels once broken down.

Wood materials are carbon-rich and use nitrogen to decompose, causing a temporary nutritional imbalance in the garden beds. However, the nitrogen imbalance is on the surface, which is positive because it doesn't feed weed seeds. Farther down in the soil the situation is normal. You can buy wood chips, shavings, and bark from sawmills and landscaping depots. The material is cheap but transport is often expensive. Mulching bark is sold bagged in plant nurseries and home improvement stores.
Usage: Wood materials are recommended for covering perennial beds but they work with mature annuals too. Smaller plants and newly sown crops can, however, drown in the heavy material. Place 1¼–2 in. (3 cm–5 cm) layers. Wood chips and bark are excellent ground cover for paths and other walking surfaces as they keep weeds and messy clay at bay. With time, it will decompose into humus that can be raked onto the beds. Sometimes fungus grows in the material. That is a good sign because it shows the soil is rich

UNNECESSARY WORRY ABOUT WOOD CHIPS

Wood chips and bark contain terpenes and phenols, chemical compounds created naturally in trees as a protection against pests and competition from other plants. Terpenes are found especially in conifers. Gardeners frequently express worry about these compounds and there are often discussions about possible harmful or toxic effects on crops. However, they have seldom posed a practical problem because the compounds break down when they come into contact with microorganisms in the soil.

in fungal mycelium.

Pros: Provides slow-acting nutrition. Retains moisture. Inhibits weed growth. Easy to work with. Perfect for covering walking paths.

Cons: Poor nutrition. Might steal nitrogen. Too slow to decompose when used in garden beds. Awkward when sowing. Might be difficult to get your hands on product. Shavings can clump together and stick to shoe soles, tools, and plants.

SHEEP'S FLEECE is rich in nutrition and covers well if it is placed in big sheets. It evens out the temperature in garden beds. It is often possible to get cotted/matted fleece for free from a sheep farmer as they can't easily treat fleece full of plant material, excrement, and other impurities.

Usage: Place in layers 2–4 in. thick (5 cm–10 cm). The fleece decomposes slowly and, as this occurs, it is acceptable to add on top of other material. Occasionally push some other organic material underneath to increase the humus content.

Pros: Provides nutrition. Covers well. Retains moisture. Blocks weeds. Increases light reflection. Is deer and rabbit resistant. Slugs don't seem to like it. Free of charge.

Cons: Difficult to find a source. Long decomposition. Awkward when direct sowing in beds.

Any kind of **COMPOST** works as a complement for other mulching materials.

Usage: Place as you get it in mulched beds. (Read more about growing in mulched beds on p. 25.)

Pros: Provides the soil with nutrition and humus. Smothers weeds. Retains moisture.

Cons: Heavy to carry especially if it is wet. Depending on compost method, it might contain perennial weeds. May be expensive.

GARDEN FABRIC, WEED BARRIERS, ROW COVERS, and **GROUND COVERS** are sometimes placed on top of other organic mulching materials in mulched beds.

Garden fabric, weed barrier, or ground covers are often used on fallow beds to protect against weeds, stop moisture from evaporating and carbon dioxide from leaking. They are sometimes used during the growing season with the plants inserted into the soil through holes cut in the fabric. Ground covers are mainly used for smothering runner weeds spreading in pathways.

How to: After harvesting, place the fabric on the bed, but first add a layer of organic mulch. The fabric is a winter cover. The fabric retains carbon dioxide and smothers weeds. Once it is time to sow in the spring, the cover is removed to show a humus-rich weed-free garden bed.

When used during the growing season, the fabric is placed on top of the garden bed that has been prepared with compost or mulch. Cut Xs in the fabric and insert the plants. Water through the holes or position a drip hose under the fabric to facilitate irrigation. When making new paths between beds, place ground cover under a walking surface made of, for example, wood chips or straw. It isn't advisable to use ground cover in garden beds because the weave shuts out the working microorganisms.

Pros: Keeps away weeds. Retains moisture. Prevents carbon dioxide leakage. Makes a clean growing surface; plants that grow through fabric are not full of dirt.

Cons: Doesn't add humus or nutrients to the soil. Some fabrics fray, let through too much light, or don't last very long. Plastic materials have a tendency to rip and scatter around the garden. Might make soil conditions too dense.

GARDEN FABRICS TO BUY—AND THEIR PROPERTIES

Fabric made of polypropylene (PP) plastic. This won't let through any light, which is good for total weed suppression. It won't let through air or water, which makes it unsuitable for growing. Will last about three to five years. Non-degradable. Recyclable.

Cover fabric from compressed polypropylene plastic fibers. Lets air and water through, as well as about 20 percent of light. Doesn't fray when cut. Lasts about two to three years. Non-degradable. Recyclable.

Ground cover strips made of polypropylene (sometimes referred to by the trademark name Mypex). Lets through light, water, and approximately 1 percent of light. Will fray if cut. May let through aggressive weeds. Will last up to ten years. Non-degradable. Recyclable.

Woven strips of agrotextile based on two biodegradable polymers. Lets through air, water, and approximately 30 percent of light. Frays if cut. May let through aggressive weeds. Biodegradability starts after about three years.

COMPOST—BEDDED DOWN FOR COMFORTABLE GROWING

Compost is often referred to as garden's gold. It's not strange when you remember that compost contributes humus and nutrition to the garden beds, while also acting as a moisture-retaining cover, and it also smothers weeds. As a result, compost is considered a mulching material, even if already decomposed when placed on the garden bed. It's a big asset that compost is made from already existing natural garden materials because it means that nothing needs to be burned or transported to a recycling facility. All in all, compost is golden and in many ways a climate-smart resource for the No-Dig garden.

Composting is all about breaking down organic materials into nutritious humus. This is done with the help of microorganisms; small insects and worms, that in a clear order of succession, devour both plant matter as well as other organisms and/or their excrement. This process produces energy, which gives off heat, which in turn, together with bacteria, can kill disease-causing elements and harmful organisms.

The basic principles of composting are simple. Various organic matters, together with water, oxygen, and heat, are the elements needed for the breakdown organisms to get quickly and efficiently to work. The heat the compost produces needs to be elevated in order to break down the disease-producing organisms. This heat requires a very large amount of materials. The compost bin or pile needs to be at least 35½ cubic ft. (i.e. 3¼ ft. x 3¼ ft. x 3¼ ft., or 1 cubic meter) to produce the necessary heat. The decomposition may take from a few months up to a few years depending on material, volume, and method.

There are a variety of composts. Around kitchen gardens we talk mostly about garden and household compost. The former builds on garden debris while the latter is food scraps and other organic kitchen materials. Livestock manure and leaves also create good compost. All compost is valuable to a No-Dig garden, so use what you can get your hands on. In the beginning, there's quite a great need for compost in order to smother weeds and prepare beds. It is sometimes necessary to buy compost if you can't or haven't got the time to make your own.

It is difficult to calculate the fertilizing effect of compost because nutritional value varies depending on the origin of the materials and also on how complete the decomposition is. However, exact nutritional values aren't especially interesting in No-Dig gardening. What is most important is to use lots of organic plant materials that your soil's inhabitants can recycle into humus, creating a natural nutrition cycle for the soil.

There are many different compost containers and various ways to process the organic materials. The methods determine where the garden or the household compost will go and how fertile it will become. The basics are always the same whichever method is used: Find the balance between carbon-rich and nitrogen-rich materials.

Nitrogen-rich materials like grass, weeds, vegetable scraps, garden debris, hay, seaweed, and livestock manure are rich in nutrition and are quickly broken down. Material rich in carbon like wood chips and shavings, cardboard, straw, and leaves contain sparse nutrition and decompose slowly but provide humus elements and structure to the soil.

A COMPOST LECTURE

Thoroughly composted compost is often called "finished" or "ripe" compost. The microorganisms have broken down all its contents, mixed carbon and nitrogen, and bound both big and small nutritional substances. Together, all organic and mineral matter produces a fresh, earthy smelling, and dark humus of high microbial activity (i.e. humus that will help to amend and build the black growing soil). (Read more in the chapter on geology on p. 138.) Thoroughly processed and stable compost works in three ways:

Physically: Increased humus content gives the soil a structure that preserves moisture and oxygen. Because of this, the plant roots have a good environment to thrive in and absorb nutrients.

Chemically: Nutrients don't disappear and aren't leached out of humus-rich soil. The store of nutrition in stable organic matter is released slowly, at a speed the plants can absorb. Increased humus content also helps the soil resist acidification.

Biologically: Microbial activity increases. Each compost ration adds microorganisms. In addition, it improves the conditions for microbial life itself. Useful microbes make life untenable for disease-causing pathogenic fungi and bacteria, mainly the ones causing soil-borne diseases.

Kitchen compost with plenty of worm activity.

A sectional view of garden compost. The bottom layer is ready for use.

FULLY PROCESSED COMPOST—HOW TO TEST

One way to test if your compost is ready to use for sowing and planting a crop is to mix a few radish or cress seeds with the compost. The compost is ready for use if the seeds germinate.

IT'S TIME TO SPREAD COMPOST

Fully processed compost can be placed on the garden bed in the fall. Nutrition in a fully processed compost is firmly bound in the organic matter, which makes it less likely to leach out into the surroundings. Not until it's warm enough for microorganisms to continue working will the compost break down to make nutrition available for the plants. Then again, you have to take climate and soil into consideration. During increasingly warmer winters, the microorganisms continue to work and release nutrition, even though there are no plants to absorb it. While clay soil retains nutrients and water well, sandy soil is less efficient at it and the nutrition risks leaking out. With this in mind, spread compost only in the fall if your soil is more clay than sand-based, and if you know that you'll have a proper winter climate. Once spring arrives, the garden bed is ready to be sown and planted. If it suits your garden's annual rhythm better, you can spread the ready compost in the spring.

Non-fully processed compost should not be placed on the garden bed in the fall. When nothing grows and can absorb the nutrients the water-soluble, quick-acting nutrition will leak which may cause eutrophication of natural waterways. Long term it will also cause a loss to future crops.

Compost occupies a central position in the No-Dig garden, especially in mulched garden beds covered with a ¾ in. (2 cm) layer of compost every fall. Mulched beds don't need fully processed compost since the mulching material is composted in place. However, compost can also be used in the same manner as other mulching materials.

Whichever composting method you choose, all organic plant matter provides soil life with food. Leave the worms, insects, and microorganisms to do their work undisturbed. They will reward you with a porous soil, complete with a clever nutritional network that will make your plants thrive.

Compost—varieties, properties, and how to create them

GARDEN COMPOST is made up of fresh and dried plants, leftover fruit, vegetable stems, leaves, and other organic plant debris. Microorganisms and insects process and break down this material into compost.

Garden compost is often referred to as cold composting, even though, when it is in the correct volume, it can become hot during the process. Garden debris can be broken down through both slow- and fast-acting processes. A slow-acting compost process demands very little effort but might take a year to break down. It'll be pretty nutrient-poor and may contain weed seeds or pathogens. A fast-acting compost process demands more work and planning, but it decomposes the material quickly and results in healthy and nutrient-rich compost. The quick-acting compost will heat up considerably and quickly, as long as it's in the correct volume. Both composts smell like soil and look brown and soil-like when fully processed.

Container: There are ready-made composters available—from simple compost bins to more expensive kinds made of plastic or wood. You can also build a bin of wooden slats, or braid one out of willow or birch branches. Three pallet collars placed on top of each other also make a good compost bin. Leave some space between the collars for airflow. The bin does not have a bottom because composting is based on worms and microorganisms being able to work up into the compost material from the soil. Compost can also consist of a simple pile on the ground. With space for two to three piles or bins, the process will become very efficient. It's very handy starting a new compost pile while a second is processing and a third one is going through the final compost-ripening stage.

Placement: Choose a spot in half shade, but not near a tree or sturdy bushes because the roots will unfailingly invade the compost.

Slow-acting garden compost

In a slow-acting garden compost the material more or less looks after itself. It works on the idea that all garden debris, when added a bit at a time, will eventually decompose. An undisturbed pile will take several years to turn into humus. It will go faster if you give it a bit of a helping hand. The trick is to add moisture and oxygen by watering and turning the material. In cold compost, *Eisenia fetida* worms do most of the breakdown work. The worms, also called compost worms, exist naturally in compost but can also be imported. Get some from the nearest compost pile or order them online. Compost worms work in cold temperatures, and are only active when the temperature is below 77°F (25°C) while fungi and bacteria work in the warm middle of the compost pile.

BE WARY OF HOUSEPLANTS

Never use plant debris or soil from professionally grown houseplants in your compost. Many houseplants are treated with paclobutrazol, a growth retardant and fungicide that ensures compact plants with profuse flowering, which is good for sales. However, paclobutrazol breaks down slowly and can have a negative effect on the kitchen garden, even if the plant debris has spent time in the compost pile. If you're not sure that your plant is free from growth retardant, don't put it in the compost pile.

MATERIALS FOR GARDEN COMPOST

Nitrogen-rich debris such as grass cuttings, hedge trimmings, fresh harvest debris, vegetables, livestock manure, green herbs, and seaweed. **Carbon-rich debris** such as wilted plant material, dried leaves, straw, hay, wood chips, sawdust, dry twigs and branches, bark, cardboard, and dry grass.

CAUTION!

Some gardeners even add plant debris that is infected with clump root disease, potato leaf mold, cotton foliar disease, potato warts, or tomato and cucumber mosaic virus to the compost. The reason being, once the material is broken down into compost the diseases won't survive because there is no plant tissue to attach to. Other gardeners choose to burn or dispose of their heavily infected plants. A tip: only place badly infected plants in the compost if you master and diligently follow up the composting process. If not, don't!

How to: Line the bottom of the bin with a 7 in. (20 cm) layer of finely chopped twigs or branches and continue to add all garden debris as it becomes available. Layer nitrogen-rich plant matter with carbon-rich matter at an approximate ratio of ⅓ fresh to ⅔ carbon-rich. The guideline here is: rather too dry material than too wet.

Finely shred the material and spread it over the whole compost surface. The material lures in the ground insects and microorganisms to start the breakdown work. Water if the layers look too dry. By checking on the compost often, you'll get the best feel for the correct mixture; make sure it has started working, and that it's neither too wet nor too dry.

The compost soil gets ready from the bottom up, making the pile sink during the composting process. Continue to replenish the pile with available material. Water if it's too dry and turn the pile occasionally to add oxygen, which accelerates the composting process.

Transfer the compost to a new location after about six months and let it work for another year. To protect against nitrogen loss, place a covering on the compost: a layer of straw, an old rug, or a piece of composting fabric works fine. The compost will be ready in about one to two years.

Pros: Produces great humus. Easy to work with. **Cons:** Nutritionally poor. Lengthy process. Demands aeration. Can contain weed seeds, wood pieces, and clods. Variable quality. Emits carbon dioxide when turned. Sometimes the compost doesn't get hot enough to kill off weed seeds and pathogens.

Quick garden compost

Quick garden compost requires both work and care, relying on the immediate availability of large amounts of materials. Nevertheless, the principle is simple: it is all about layering dry carbon-rich material with nitrogen-rich fresh material, preferably shredded into smaller pieces. It also requires both moisture and oxygen.

The compost volume needs to be at least a cubic foot (i.e. the bottom of the composting pile has to be at least 10¾ sq. ft. [1 m2], and the height at least 3¼ ft. [1 meter]), for the material to retain moisture and heat. The temperature increases during the process as the bacteria, worms, and other microbes go to work on the material. The compost will work best at 149°F (65°C), which is when both weed seeds and harmful pathogens die. When the compost temperature decreases to 104°F–131°F (40°C–55°C) the rest of the materials are broken down further. The worms and other larger soil workers retreat when the temperature increases, and they return when it gets cooler to release nutrients and build humus.

How to: Have enough material on hand to fill the compost bin/pile in one go. Cover the bottom with a layer of finely shredded twigs and branches. Continue to layer nitrogen-rich garden debris with carbon-rich at a ratio of 1:3 green to 2:3 carbon-rich materials. Pile dry and fresh material in thin layers so the worms are able to access both equally. Kick-start the process by adding some livestock manure, a splash of urine, or already existing compost to the middle of the pile. Water between the layers. When the bin is full, or the pile large enough, the compost will be working and in a few days it can have reached 149°F (65°C).

TIPS AGAINST WEED INVASION AND DISEASES

• To make sure that there won't be any viable seeds in the finished compost, place all plant material with seeds in their own composting container. Make sure the compost reaches high enough temperature to kill off the seeds. If you do put seeds in compost that is not closely monitored, deposit them into the middle to be sure they really get hot and die.

• Place perennial runner-propagated weeds like couch grass, ground elder, and thistle in their own container to wither and dry before they are added to the compost. It also works to place them in the sun to dry.

• Most viruses, fungal diseases, harmful bacteria, and noxious weeds die in temperatures above 131°F (55°C), so it is often possible to add noxious plants to the compost. Place the troublesome plants in the middle, make sure that the compost temperature rises like it should, and turn over the compost once a year to renew the process. Make sure the outer layer is moved inwards so the heat works on all plant debris.

FOR AND AGAINST COMPOSTING

Compost has been targeted lately as an environmental hazard as it emits greenhouse gases, especially carbon dioxide, when it is being turned and aerated.

This is however not a reason to stop composting because it's just as bad not to recuperate garden debris or household food scraps. The picture of compost as an environmental baddie can also be modified by the insight that all other breakdown of organic matter emits gases. Humans for example emit gases constantly; from exhaling to how we run our industries.

There are tricks to make composting environmentally friendly:

• Gardening in mulched beds means that the soil inhabitants (which, by the way, also breathe and emit gases) break down the organic matter into humus directly in the beds. Because of this, turning the compost is superfluous.

• Greenhouse gas emission can be controlled if the moisture level is kept low during the most active phase. Make sure, though, that the compost doesn't dry out during the latter part of the process.

• Use the compost as soon as possible when it is ready.

Place a cover over the compost to counteract leaching, to reduce gas emissions, and to preserve the heat. Anything from a tarpaulin or an old rug, to a layer of straw will work. Keep an eye on the interior temperature by placing a wooden pole down the middle of the pile; that way you can regularly check how the temperature is doing. Pull up the pole and check how warm it is. The working temperature is perfect if the touch burns; it will cool down as the compost stabilizes. There are thermometers for sale in plant nurseries if you want to know the exact temperature.

Depending on the organic mixture and volume, the compost will cool down in a few days or a few months. When the temperature reaches 95°F–104°F (35°C–40°C) it's time to add oxygen. The simplest way is to move the compost into another container. At the same time, adjust the ratio between dry and fresh materials. Water as needed. Once the compost has been turned, the temperature may suddenly start rising again. Stir and water, or stamp on the compost, to make it cool down again. Let the compost process fully. Protect it with some kind of cover. The compost will be ready in three to six months.

Pros: Nutrient-rich. Quick to make. Produces good humus.

Cons: Demands lots of material in one go. Needs guarding and aeration. Emits carbon dioxide when turned. Emits ammonia if the temperature goes above 158°F (70°C).

HOUSEHOLD COMPOST, also called warm compost, is made from kitchen waste. It uses both cooked food leftovers and other organic household waste. Household compost is very nutritious. Kitchen waste is usually very nitrogen-rich, so it needs to be mixed with litter to get the

A composter often takes enormous pleasure in seeing organic debris transform into rich humus.

LITTER FOR HOUSEHOLD COMPOST

Wood shavings, wood chips, straw, bark, dry leaves, household paper, ripped up paper egg cartons, shredded newspaper.

right balance between carbon and nitrogen. Litter protects the mix from getting too wet. To compost household waste you need a closed container or the compost will attract vermin. To get permission to compost household waste it is often necessary to inform the local authorities of your intent. Always check your local laws.

Container: You can buy special containers for household compost. A container with a rotating drum eliminates the need for stirring the compost and makes the material break down quickly. It needs to be a closed container so the content doesn't attract vermin and pests. It should also allow for at least 13¼ gallons (50 liters) of waste material per person in the household. A good container is pest-safe and has circulation through both the bottom and the lid because oxygen is necessary for effective composting. To be on the safe side, use extra precaution against rats and field mice by attaching plastering mesh netting (i.e. a galvanized mesh square with maximum ⅜ in. (10 mm) holes in the bottom) with a ratchet strap around the container.

The container also needs drainage at the bottom to allow excess water created during the composting process, called leachate, to run off. If it is to be used during the winter, the container needs to be insulated. Make sure the container is easily opened in order to add material and to later empty out the completed compost. Ideally, two containers are used, one for composting and one for the final processing. Material that is completely broken down can be finished in a pile on the ground or in sacks with ventilation holes.

Placement: Place near the kitchen so the waste actually ends up in the container. Place the container on a flat surface and in a location where it gets some shade.

How to: Start with a 4–7 in. (10 cm–2 cm) layer of finely chopped twigs as they contribute to drainage and air flow (this is not needed with a rotating drum container). Pour in a bucketful of garden soil or processed compost, which contains plenty of microorganisms to kick-start the breakdown process. Successively add food waste; it needs to be finely shredded for the process to work. Make sure to mix in litter at a ratio of 1 part litter to 1 part waste. Stir with a pole, or rotate if using a rotating container. While the compost processes the temperature might reach 140°F (60°C). Stir the compost or rotate the container once a week to aerate. Add material and litter until the container is full. The compost is ready when it starts to cool down and is dark and crumbly. Let the compost ripen in the container or in a pile on the ground for about two to three months, or the same amount of time as it has been in the container.

Pros: Full of nutrition. Produces very nice humus. Quick to make.

Cons: Need to use a securely closed container.

LEAF COMPOST produces very fine and moisture-retaining humus with good structure. It is simple to compost leaves but it is a long process. Leaf compost is nutritionally poor.

Container: Leaves are composted in a pile on the ground or in an open-bottom container. If you haven't got the room or don't want the pile out in the open, it works just as well to compost leaves in plastic sacks with holes for air circulation. The sacks won't have true contact with the soil, but it still works very well because microorganisms have already colonized the leaves fallen on the ground. The temperature also increases in the sack; especially if nitrogen-rich material, which has a positive effect on the decomposition, is added.

Placement: Place it in a secluded corner where a compost pile, bin, or sacks will not offend your aesthetic sensibilities.

How to: Collect leaves and place them in a pile on the ground or in an open-bottom compost bin, or in plastic sacks. Oak and beech leaves take a long time to decompose; finely shred them with the lawn mower before composting. Add some livestock manure to give a helping hand with the

NEVER PUT THIS IN THE HOUSEHOLD COMPOST
Snuff, cigarette ends
Diapers
Sanitary towels, tampons
Cat litter, dog excrement
Vacuum cleaner bags
Chewing gum
Chalk
Waxed or plasticized paper
Textiles
Twigs, sticks
Large quantities of soil from
    houseplants and ornamentals

. . . BUT DO PUT THESE IN
Food scraps
Fruit and vegetables,
    including peel and leftovers
Bread, cookies
Coffee grounds, tea leaves,
    coffee filters, teabags made
    of paper
Chicken and meat (avoid
    larger bones)
Fish, fish guts and trimmings,
    shrimp and crawfish shells
Flour, rice, pasta
Dairy products
Egg, crushed eggshells
Popcorn, chips, sweets and
    candy
Paper towel, napkins
Withered flowers
Dried sawdust
Garden debris
Biochar

PROBLEMS IN THE COMPOST AND HOW TO SOLVE THEM

Problem	Explanation	Solution
The process doesn't start. The compost temperature is not high enough and the process has stopped.	Not enough materials. Materials too dry. Winter cold. Not enough variety in materials.	Add more of both nitrogen-rich and dry materials. Water. Stir the compost. Add fresh livestock manure or add urine to the compost.
Temperature too high.	Too much oxygen.	Stamp down on the compost to press out the oxygen.
Ammonia odor.	Nitrogen level too high. Temperature too high.	Add dry carbon-rich material. Turn the compost. Stamp down on the compost to release oxygen.
Smells like rot.	Badly aerated and compacted. Too much nitrogen-rich material, which rots in oxygen-poor environments.	Stir the compost to aerate. Add coarser, carbon-rich material and stir again.
Ants	The pile/container is too dry.	Water, stir/turn the material.
Flies and larvae.	Temperature too low. Alternative—too much nitrogen-rich material and too little oxygen so the material rots and attracts flies.	Add nitrogen-rich material to raise the temperature. Alternative—add carbon-rich material to the rotting nitrogen material. Stir after adding the new material. Otherwise, larvae in ripening compost are good for breakdown, so leave them alone.

breakdown, or layer with windfall, which attracts a lot of worms. Water. Turn the compost with a pitchfork now and then. If the leaves are composted in a plastic sack they need to be watered before the sack is tied together. Also add some livestock manure or urine. Make a few holes in the sack with a pitchfork to let in both air and microorganism. Put it aside and wait. The compost will be ready in 18–24 months.

Pros: Produces lots of good, fine, and loose structured humus. No clods. Large amount of fungus hyphae.

Cons: Low nutritional value. Time consuming.

LIVESTOCK COMPOST is the same as very-well-ripened livestock manure (i.e. droppings and urine from a cow or horse), often mixed with litter. (We normally place composted sheep, goat, pig, and hen droppings under the label livestock compost but we're only talking about cow and horse compost here because it produces larger volumes.)

Manure needs to compost for nearly two years to be properly processed. However, it is possible to produce nutrient-rich and ready farm compost in between six months and a year if it is turned/rotated regularly.

The original raw material—livestock manure—contains nitrogen, phosphorus, potassium, and many micronutrients. Don't confuse composted manure with fresh or cured manure as the latter has not been composted as long and therefore has different effects in the garden. (Read more about livestock manure's stages on the next page spread.)

Droppings and litter are broken down during composting through a heat-producing process. Any harmful bacteria and any weed seed that might have been in the litter also die. Depending on volume, the temperature can reach 158°F (70°C)—the heat is proof positive that the manure is processing. After this the temperature gradually tapers off. It will take up to half a year until the manure is processed, and then the breakdown into compost continues.

Both cow and horse compost deliver plenty of good nutrition. They also provide structure to the soil if the original manure was mixed with litter. Both add rich microbial life and contain a balanced nutrient level. It's possible to direct sow and plant in livestock compost, as long as it is properly aged and therefore low in nutrition. Livestock manure with high nitrogen levels risks burning small roots and root stems.

Horse manure is often free from a riding school or from a farmer. If you look after your compost and get the temperature up high enough, deworming products and antibiotic residue pose no threats as they are broken down during the composting process. If you're unsure how high your compost temperature goes, leave manure containing pharmaceutical residue alone. Preferably choose manure mixed with organic straw. Bagged composted livestock manure is even sold in plant nurseries and box stores. It is labeled cow manure and is usually cow manure compost mixed with peat.

Container/bin: Livestock manure can be stored piled on the ground or in an open compost bin.

Placement: Choose somewhere secluded in the garden so neither your neighbors nor you are bothered by manure smells and flies.

How to: Place the manure in a pile on the ground, or in an open-ended compost bin, to allow the microbial life to enter straight in and go to work. The material composts slowly and without any handling, except perhaps an occasional watering and aeration. You'll accelerate the process and conserve nutrition by using the compost regularly. Cover the pile with straw or garden fabric. The cover protects against weather and wind which otherwise causes the nutrition to leach out. Water as needed or remove the cover in rainy weather if the compost is too dry.

The completed compost is free of odor, has the same temperature as the surroundings, and has a crumbly texture. The compost will be ready in 18–24 months, or 6–12 if you turn it regularly.

Pros: Humus-rich, with an even nutritional level. Nutrient-rich in shorter compost time. Adds microorganisms. Easy to handle. You can sow and plant directly in old compost.

Cons: Relatively nutrient poor if it has been composted over a long period. May contain weed seed.

BOKASHI is a Japanese method that makes it possible to compost a variety of kitchen waste, without it causing bad odors or attracting flies. Everything from vegetable debris, fruit, and bread

THE VARIOUS STAGES OF LIVESTOCK MANURE

Fresh livestock manure is rich in nutrition and humus elements. The nutrition quickly becomes water-soluble and may leak out if nothing binds or absorbs it. Horse manure usually contains plenty of carbon materials like straw, wood chips, or peat. Nitrogen is used to break down the material's carbon content during the decomposing process. If fresh manure is placed directly in the garden beds the breakdown process can dip into the existing nitrogen in the soil. Of course, nitrogen is released again once the carbon is broken down, but in the meanwhile the bedding plants suffer nutritionally. Manure has to be free of carbon-rich materials if it is to be used fresh. However, it is rather too strong for fragile plant roots in the spring and high nutrition levels may make plants more susceptible to disease and pests. Moreover, the taste and shelf life of fruits and vegetables may be impaired. Fresh, unfinished manure usually smells and gives off heat when the pile is aerated. Fresh manure is primarily used to establish garden beds, and is then complemented with carbon-rich materials. It can also be mixed with water and be used as a fertilizer boost if the plants look malnourished. (Find recipe on p. 121.)

Processed livestock manure has gone through a heat-generating breakdown process that results in a material free of pathogens, weed seed, and possible drug residue. The manure is processed when the temperature cools but the decomposing continues for another six (6) months. Processed livestock manure has a sturdier structure than fresh, and a lower but more balanced level of nutrition that won't leach out. Well-done manure has the appearance of soil and is of the same temperature as the surroundings. This, combined with other materials, is used to build garden beds.

Ripe or **composted** livestock manure is processed manure that has been composted for a year. Composted livestock manure has low, but balanced, nutritional levels and has the appearance of finely crumbled humus. It is used for the preparation of garden beds and also as mulching material. One part composted horse manure mixed with two parts leaf compost makes a great planting soil.

LUSCIOUS LEACHATE

The liquid collected at the bottom of the Bokashi bucket contains nutrition and leftover good microorganisms. You can tap some excellent fertilizing liquid from a Bokashi bucket fitted with a spigot. The liquid is very potent and needs to be diluted with water at a ratio of 1:100. Leachate often smells bad but the result makes it all worth it.

to fish scales and meat bones can be put into Bokashi compost. The method is to place the waste in an airtight bucket where you layer with efficient microorganisms (EM). Microorganisms help to ferment food waste and when the material is later mixed with soil it transforms to humus in just a few weeks. The humus is highly nutritious thanks to the working microorganisms that split the proteins from the kitchen waste into amino acids that the plants can use immediately.

Bokashi is usually buried in the ground, but for No-Dig gardening the material can be mixed with soil in a closed but ventilated bucket, box, barrel, or pallet collar. It becomes a kind of soil factory in which the bokashi compost takes on soil form, which can later be spread across the gardening bed. There is less risk of vermin interfering with this closed soil factory.

The bokashi compost can also be layered in the gardening bed. It is placed directly on the bed and is covered by soil, leaves, straw, and other organic materials. It's wise to place a compost grid on top to stop curious animals from having a closer look. The conversion to soil happens in a few weeks during summer but the colder it gets the longer it takes. Freezing weather doesn't harm the process. Warmer weather will restart it.

Container: There are specially designed containers for sale that come with a sieve and a spigot for recuperating the precious leachate. However, it is just as easy to use common household buckets if the bottom is layered with biochar, egg cartons, or newspapers to soak up the leachate, avoiding bad odors. It is important to have a tight-fitting lid on your bucket because the method relies on an oxygen-free atmosphere to ferment the waste.

Accessories: Bokashi bran, commonly wheat bran that has been grafted with a variety of efficient microorganisms (EM), or liquid bokashi spray, can be found in plant nurseries or online. A closed but ventilated container, for example, a garbage can with a lid slightly ajar, is also needed to use as a soil factory.

Placement: Under the sink if indoors. It can also be placed outdoors.

How to: Spread a few tablespoons of bokashi bran on the bottom of the container, or rinse it with a dose of bokashi spray. If using a bucket, place a layer of newspaper on the bottom. Add some crushed grill charcoal or biochar for even better results.

Add the waste, preferably broken up into smaller pieces. Sprinkle over a few tablespoons of bokashi bran per quart (1 liter) of waste, or one or two squirts of bokashi spray. Press the material down hard with a compactor or potato masher. The method works on the principle the bucket maintains an oxygen-free atmosphere; so don't lift the lid unnecessarily. Collect food waste in a smaller container with a lid to prevent flies from depositing their eggs in the waste. Move the waste to the bokashi container once a day and replace the lid carefully. Once it's full, the container needs to rest for two weeks at room temperature. This is when the fermenting process happens. After it's fermented, the material is moved to the larger soil factory container. The material will have the same structure as when it was moved to the bokashi container. It's not until now the conversion to soil starts. Cover the bottom of the soil factory with some old soil or dry leaves, place the fermented food waste on top and mix it with soil. Cover with another 4 in. (10 cm) of soil or leaves. Do *not* stir! When oxygen enters the process, some of the carbon is converted to carbon dioxide and methane. It's better that the energy is used in the soil rather than emitted into the air. At room temperature, or outside during the summer, it will take two weeks for the material to turn into soil; four weeks total from filled container to completed humus. The process will take longer in the winter.

Pros: Good nutritional level. Quick to make. Can be made indoors.
Cons: Does not turn into soil immediately; requires several steps. Can become really malodorous if there is too much oxygen entering the container, if the bokashi bran is too old, or if the material is wet or not shredded finely enough.

MUSHROOM COMPOST is the remnants after mushroom cultivation (usually champignons). The growers use the compost approximately three times and then it is unusable for mushroom growing. However, it's great for gardening. The compost is a mix of horse and chicken manure, wheat straw, and fungal mycelium. It provides lots of nutrition, is good for microbial life, and contributes humus elements. The compost is cheap but not always organic as some growers use pesticides that do not break down in the process. Check if the compost contains these chemical contaminants before you collect.

Pros: Contributes humus elements. No weed seed or debris. Easy to handle. Relatively cheap.

Cons: Unreliable or low nutritional content. Microbial life is disturbed. Expensive transport. Might contain chemical residues.

COMPOST FROM RECYCLING FACILITIES (ie. garden debris and/or horse manure), processed in either communal or private composting facilities, can provide great humus for the garden. This kind of compost is sold directly from facilities, often by the truckload or in large sacks. Certain facilities "hygienize" the compost, which means it's heated and subjected to pressure, reducing and killing pathogens. The process affects the nutritional value and the microorganisms negatively; but on the other hand, the compost will most certainly be more or less weed free. In most places, unless the compost is marked organic, it might contain chemicals, depending on where the source material came from.

Home delivery of compost is very expensive; however, it's cheap if you collect it yourself. Check with your local authorities to see if they produce compost and how to collect it. The compost is ready to use immediately.

Pros: Adds humus. There are no weed seeds or weed residues. Easy to handle. Easy on the pocketbook.

Cons: Uncertain or low nutritional value. The microorganisms have been disturbed. High home delivery cost. Might contain chemical residue.

NUTRITION

Fertilizers are usually given large importance in a gardening book. In No-Dig gardening, no extra fertilizing is needed except at the start-up phase or with very intensive cultivation.

It is still important that, as a grower, you understand how different nutrients and fertilizers work. You can then give the microbial life a helping hand before the soil has learned to look after itself. If your beds look like they need a bit of a nutritional boost, you don't risk standing there clueless.

FERTILIZERS—KINDS AND THEIR EFFECTS

The general rule is that it takes about three years of mulched bed gardening to get a soil with weak microbial life up to scratch. Before a newly created garden bed has worked itself into natural nutritional self-sufficiency, it is grateful for any boost given; like a kick-start to up the nutritional level. If you change the system from Dig to No-Dig gardening a nutritional distribution imbalance might develop, which makes it necessary to fertilize. Perhaps certain demanding crops like cabbage and leeks could use a dose of fertilizer. If you grow several crops during the season in one location you might need to boost the soil. On the following pages we'll look at some fertilizers that are convenient to have on hand.

Solid fertilizers

Horse manure contains all the nutrients plants need. It can be used in various ways: *Fresh horse manure* is often mixed with some kind of bedding material that the animals stood in. These materials (wood shavings, straw, etc.) are rich in carbon and are broken down with the help of nitrogen in the animal droppings. Fresh manure placed directly in the garden bed might bind nitrogen from the soil when decomposing, causing a lack of nutrients rather than giving the soil a boost. Counteract this by adding nitrogen, for example: grass clippings or nitrogen-rich fertilizer liquid. *Processed* or *composted horse manure* produces fine structure and nutrition. It's mild and difficult to overdose, and is used as mulch or compost.

Cow manure has all nutrients plants need and is especially rich in potassium. *Fresh cow manure* is seldom used directly in beds because it's too sticky to handle. *Processed* or *composted cow manure* is easier to deal with and produces a long-lasting fertilizing effect. Bagged cow manure is composted and often mixed with peat. (Read more about the various stages of livestock manure on p. 113.)

Chicken manure contributes, primarily, easily absorbed nitrogen but also contains high levels of phosphorus. *Fresh chicken manure* is more potent than horse and cow manure and should be used in small doses due to the risk of overdosing and leaching. *Composted chicken manure* is preferred rather than fresh. *Dried* or *pelleted chicken manure*, sold in plant nurseries, is very concentrated and should be used according to the instructions on the packaging.

Bone meal contains calcium, phosphorus, and nitrogen. This is a slow-acting fertilizer made from the bones of slaughtered animals.

Blood meal contains lots of nitrogen. A quick-acting fertilizer made of dried and pulverized blood from slaughtered animals.

Rock dust is the leftover from crushed stone (macadam) manufacturing. Contains potassium and phosphorus; levels depend on where the stone was quarried. Slow-acting.

Fresh grass clippings aren't just good, humus-rich mulching material but work very well as fertilizer. Grass cuttings have all the nutrients plants need and in the exact right proportions too. The breakdown happens at a speed that delivers the nutrition when the plants need it.

Liquid fertilizers

Nettle water is a quick-acting panacea giving the soil nitrogen, phosphorus, potassium, and all the minerals you can think of. Make a nettle solution by filling a 2½ gallon (approx. 10 liters) bucket with nettles and then pour on water. Place a lid on the bucket, and let the mixture soak for a week, then strain out the nettles from the liquid. A practical way to do this is to collect the nettles in netting or an old pillowcase (i.e. create a huge teabag) to avoid having to strain them later. Mix one part nettle liquid with nine parts water. Nettle water is rotted material and the smell is nasty. Water after it has rained to lessen the odor a bit. It's possible to make fermented nettle water, which doesn't smell quite as bad. You'll need to add 1⅓ cup of bottled Effective Microorganisms (EM) and 1⅓ cup of cane sugar molasses to a 2½-gallon bucket. Fermented nettle solution is more nutrient-rich than the rotted variety; so mix one part with 50–100 parts water. The nettles you recuperate afterwards can go on the garden bed or in the compost.

Comfrey water contains a large amount of potassium and lots of minerals and trace elements. Make it the same way as nettle water.

Urine or **gold water** is made from human urine. It is rich in nitrogen, potassium, and phosphorus and makes a perfect liquid fertilizer. It's calculated that a human's urine is sufficient to fertilize all the vegetables a person eats during a year. Mix one part urine with nine parts water. Any pharmaceutical residue in the urine will soon break down in the soil, so the estimated risk for using the urine is minimal. Stop gold water fertilizing a few weeks before harvesting any edibles.

Manure water (i.e. livestock compost which has soaked in water) is an all-round fertilizer. It's a good booster for tomatoes and cucumber plants during fruiting. Mix one part manure with two (2) parts water in a bucket and leave the mixture for a week. Stir this every day. Strain and dilute the concentrate until it has the color of weak tea.

COVER CROP/GREEN FERTILIZER ON FALLOW BEDS

If you suddenly find yourself with an empty garden bed, take the opportunity to boost it with green fertilizer/cover crop (i.e. plants that, through their own cycle, catch nutrition from the soil and convert it into a lush green forage crop that returns nutrition to the soil).

One special characteristic of cover crop plants is the sturdy root systems they develop if allowed to grow in the same place for two to four years. The roots grow down deep to fetch nutrition. In doing so, they loosen the soil and leave tunnels as well as fine humus material in the ground.

Green cover crop plants that only grow one season don't have time to develop deep reaching roots. They will still pick up nutrition and contribute with a green forage crop, becoming nutrient-rich and a filling mulching material. Growing a green cover crop prevents leaching by retaining the soil's humidity, and it keeps away weeds.

Sunflowers, Blue Tansy, Common Vetch, Alfalfa, Scarlet Clover, Hop Trefoil, White Clover, Subterranean Clover, and Yellow Sweet Clover are all good green cover crop/fertilizer plants. Scythe or cut them down before they set seed to prevent them from returning in full force next year.

Biochar—a nutrition-loaded soil amendment

Biochar is an old, but relatively newly rediscovered, asset that produces loose, nutrient-rich soil, or *terra preta*. "Black soil," as the Portuguese call it.

Biochar is manufactured from wood or harvest debris. This is heated in an oxygen-free environment until it reaches such high temperature the debris is broken down without burning up. The process is called pyrolysis. The charred material can absorb and retain moisture and nutrients. This makes the carbon a perfect mix of soil amendment and fertilizer. The microbial life in the ground thrives in the black soil. The carbon breaks down extremely slowly. The half-life is several thousand years, which decreases the level of carbon dioxide in the atmosphere. In this way, the biochar works as an effective carbon emission reducer.

Biochar is not a fertilizer per se. To act as one it needs to be loaded up with nutrition. Without this loading, it will instead steal nutrition from the soil. Urine and nettle water are excellent nutritional sources, as is livestock manure and compost. Half a bucket of liquid fertilizer is poured over half a bucket of finely crushed biochar. Leave this mixture for a few weeks to allow the biochar to absorb a maximum of nutrition. Solid fertilizer mixes with finely crushed biochar in a bucket at a ratio of five parts manure or compost to one part biochar. Let the mixture rest one week.

The nutrient-filled biochar is usually dug into the soil. In a No-Dig garden bed you'll place it instead on the bed and rake it

Biochar charged with nutrition becomes a
soil amendment with fertilizing effect.

about 4 in. (10 cm) into the soil. You'll need approximately just over one (1) gallon (5 liters) or 2¼ lb. (1 kg) of nutritionally charged biochar per 10¾ sq. ft. (1 m2).

Then cover as usual with compost and/or mulch material and the carbon will be recharged with nutrients. If the vegetative growth looks to lag, the carbon might already have pinched nutrition from the plants. If that's the case, give an extra boost with liquid fertilizer.

A super smart way to use biochar in No-Dig gardening: Finely shred the biochar (with a chipper if you can). Then place the shredded biochar in the compost where it will absorb lots of nutrition. When you later spread compost on the beds, the biochar comes along too.

Once the biochar is in the soil, it will distribute nutrition to hungry roots at the appropriate time as needed, ensuring the nutrients don't leach and there's no eutrophication of nearby water sources.

Biochar already charged with nutrients is sometimes sold in plant nurseries. Check the bags to find out which kind you have. Some communities manufacture their own biochar and then sell it cheaply to residents. You can also make your own.

HOW TO MAKE YOUR OWN BIOCHAR

Place firewood in a large, lidded metal container—a thoroughly cleaned paint can, for example. Make two or three holes in the lid. Place the container in a fire, outdoors or in a fireplace indoors. When you can see a welding flame through the holes in the lid everything vaporizes except the pure carbon. Open the can once it has cooled down. If it smells of tar, it needs another round in the fire. If there is no tar smell, the biochar is ready to be crushed and saturated with nutrition.

To make a larger quantity of biochar, you'll have to dig a hole in the ground. It's also possible to make a fire in an old bathtub outdoors. Place firewood in the bottom and light it. The sides prevent oxygen from reaching the fire, and everything except the pure carbon vaporizes. Once the fire has burned down to embers, douse it with water. What's left in the tub is biochar.

ARTIFICIAL FERTILIZER = NO!

Don't use artificial fertilizer! The manufacturing uses up the earth's natural resources and it doesn't benefit microbial life or the soil's humus content.

NUTRIENTS AND HOW THEY WORK

Different nutrients benefit plants in different ways. Nutrition exists naturally in everything from livestock manure and household compost to grass cuttings, urine, and in the soil itself. Nutrients are separated into macro and micro nutrition.

MACRO NUTRITION is the nutrients the plants use most. The three most important are nitrogen, phosphorus, and potassium. In addition, even calcium, magnesium, and sulfur are of importance. This is how macro nutrition works:

Nitrogen (N) allows the plant to build proteins that provide vegetative growth, shoots, and leaves. Nitrogen is found in, for example, fully processed livestock manure, in hen manure, kitchen compost, fresh grass cuttings, and urine.

Phosphorus (P) plays an important part in the plant's energy metabolism. It's part of building blocks in proteins and genetic material and promotes growth, flower formation, and fruit setting. Phosphorus is found in fully processed livestock manure, bone meal, and urine. Sometimes soil has enough naturally occurring phosphorous that you don't need to add any. Often humus soil contains plenty of available phosphorus. In soil with higher pH levels the phosphorus might be less available for the plants. (Read about pH levels on p. 136.)

Potassium (K) is important for water balance in the plant, for flower formation and fruit setting, as well as for flavor and freshness/shelf life. Potassium is found in fully processed livestock manure and urine. A large amount of potassium might also be found in the soil. Clay soils, especially, have an ability to deliver potassium to plants through the soil's moisture.

Calcium (Ca) contributes to the plant's ability to build cell walls, strengthen the plant's immune system, and increases the soil's pH. Most mineral soils contain enough calcium. Calcium can also be found in organic matter. As long as the soil is mulched there is seldom a lack of calcium.

Magnesium (Mg) is important for the creation of chlorophyll, the substance that gives the plants their green color. Magnesium also provides stability, affects water and energy transport in the plant, and stimulates seed setting. With good magnesium availability the plants can also access phosphorus more easily. Magnesium is bound, for example, to the minerals biotite and augit and is soluble in the soil moisture. There is plenty of magnesium in clay soils, less in sand- and humus-containing soils. Since magnesium exists in organic matter there is seldom a lack in mulched beds.

Sulfur (S) is part of the plant's proteins and it is important for growth. Sulfur also balances the process that creates nitrate. Sulfur exists naturally in the soil. Soils low in humus and clay content may lack sulfur. Sulfur is found in organic matter. So, as long as the soil is mulched, a lack of sulfur is hardly ever a problem for the gardener.

Micronutrients are minerals or trace minerals like zinc, iron, copper, boron, manganese, nickel, chlorine, and molybdenum. These are called micronutrients because the plants need them in such extremely small quantities. Usually the soil contains enough micronutrients. They are found in all fertilizers, and not least in broken down mulching materials and compost.

NUTRITIONAL PROBLEMS—SIGNS AND TREATMENTS

Signs of deficiency	Treatment	Signs of excess	Treatment
The leaves are small and pale. Older leaves are gold-colored and drop prematurely. Woody stems, lilac-colored stems and leaves. Long roots, white and badly branched. Stress-induced early flowering.	Add grass cuttings, water with gold or nettle water.	The plant grows too fast, becomes loose in structure and is easily attacked by diseases and pests. The leaves become large and bluish green. Inferior flowering and fruiting. Crops like spinach, lettuce, and beets develop an unhealthy nitrate content.	Reduce fertilizing. If mulching beds, reduce the fresh grass cuttings and balance with carbon-rich materials.
Slow growth, the leaves are small, hard, and bent downwards. Flower and fruit setting stops. The roots grow large while above-ground parts are small. Older leaves get red/lilac streaks, the whole plant turns a dark green color. The deficiency might be caused by low pH, as phosphorus then binds to the soil and becomes unavailable to the plant.	Add composted livestock manure and/or bone meal. Add mulch. Water. Lack of water will stop the plant's transport of phosphorus from the soil to the leaves.	Overall stunted growth. Extreme excess might cause lack of iron, calcium, manganese, and zinc. This is seldom a problem as the nutrient binds to the soil.	This is a rare problem. The only treatment is to continue to add compost and/or mulch with organic matter.
Inferior growth. Dead spots along leaf edges and leaf tips. Inferior leaf elasticity during drought. The plant droops and is susceptible to diseases. Inferior quality of fruit.	Add livestock manure compost, stone meal or gold water.	Less growth. Older leaves turn yellow-green and streaky. This is very rare but an excess can cause lack of calcium and magnesium.	A rare problem. Continue with compost and/or mulching.
Young leaves and leaf tips wither away. The leaves get burnt edges. The plant stops growing, becomes bushy, and gets smaller leaves. Pistil rot on tomato plants. Head forming plants like cabbage and lettuce rot from the interior.	This is seldom caused by a lack in the soil but by an imbalance between calcium and other nutrients that leads to the plant being unable to access the calcium. Rotting pistils is usually a sign of lack of regular watering which causes a lack of calcium. Continue to mulch and/or compost the beds. Water the soil more regularly.	Matte green color on leaves. Inferior growth.	Excess blocks the availability of phosphorus, iron, manganese, boron, zinc, copper, magnesium, and nickel. Continue to mulch and/or compost the beds. Don't use lime or lime-containing fertilizers. Possibly add non-limed peat humus.
Older leaves turn blotchy or mottled, the leaves yellow between the veins. Leaves drop prematurely.	This is caused by competition between nitrogen and potassium, and from low pH value. Correct the pH with continued mulch and/or compost on beds.	Burnt leaves. Decreased uptake of calcium and potassium with growth disturbance as a result. Very unusual.	Rare problem. Continue to mulch and/or compost the beds.
Protein building diminishes and the plant dies off. Increased nitrate content. Younger leaves grow upright, dented and yellowed between the leaf veins. Dry leaf tips. Cabbage plants may have red discolorations.	A lack of sulfur hasn't been a modern-day problem because of industrial emissions. After 1990, however, the emission of sulfur dioxide has diminished and the need to add sulfur has increased. Especially affected are soils with low humus and clay content. Continue to mulch and/or cover with compost. Add grass cuttings. Add commercial fertilizer with high sulfur level.	Older leaves become yellowish green and get reddish violet spots. Very rare.	A rare problem. Continue with compost and/or mulching.

SOIL ORGANISMS—
THE GARDENER'S
TEAMMATES

Gardeners often talk about growing plants, but the more you grow things, the more you become aware that it's the soil and its inhabitants that you should pamper. The soil is a vital part of an ecosystem where the plants themselves contribute with both nutrition and humus. Where everything from fungi and bacteria, to tiny insects and worms, work to keep everything in tip-top shape so things can live and grow. Just a single teaspoon of healthy soil contains more living organisms than there are inhabitants on our planet. The soil organisms break off nutrients and convert organic materials to porous, moisture-retaining humus. They also aerate the soil so oxygen, water, and nutrition can flow freely.

Once you get to know them, you won't want to inflict the earthquake-like upheaval of digging up your teammates below the soil surface. Give them food, water, and oxygen (plus peace and quiet) and the tiny team benefactors will pay back with fine nutritious soil in which your plants can grow abundantly.

Life underground

Fungi can be described as the soil's army of heroes. Fungi—and we're not talking about chanterelles and death caps here, but rather thin threads—lead the decomposing work in the soil. The fungi make nutrition out of everything; from wood and cellulose to dead insects and available animal carcasses. They also very quickly spread their winding threads (i.e. hyphae) into an extensive network of mycelium, transporting the nutrients from their origin over long distances to reach needy plant roots.

Soils that are dominated by fungi retain nutrients and moisture well. They also have extremely good resistance to troubles like flooding or droughts. No-Dig gardening is perfect for fungi as they thrive in undisturbed soil.

Fungal hyphae aren't visible to the naked eye until they've collected into ranks of hundreds of thousands of hyphae. Then we can see them as white lines in the soil.

Bacteria are invisible to the eye but perform a fantastic job in the soil. To start with, they grab nutrients from everything from green plants to stones. Some of them can also secure nitrogen from the air. Bacteria also secrete mucus that clumps together soil particles to grainy units which makes the soil porous and lets through water, nutrients, and oxygen.

The bacteria's enthusiastic work gives the nutrients they catch and release a slightly positive charge, which makes it easy for plants to get at them.

Bacteria want humid environments to thrive in. Some, called obligate aerobic bacteria, also need oxygen. Others detest oxygen and are called anaerobic. Pathogenic bacteria are usually anaerobic.

Protozoa are small one-celled organisms with names like ciliates, amoebas, and flagellates. Protozoans are admittedly tiny but can be seen with the naked eye. They appear as anything from see-through cell bags to $\frac{1}{16}$ in. (2 mm) elongated grains with antennas. Protozoans can't take up nourishment from either organic or non-organic matter, so they munch on bacteria and fungi to release nutrients. If suddenly there's a lack of bacteria and fungal hyphae, the protozoans will cannibalize each other while waiting for bacteria and fungi to regenerate.

Nematodes or **roundworms** are bigger than protozoa but still difficult to see without a microscope. Nematodes are the second-largest animal group on the planet. More than 20,000 mapped species exist, and it's estimated there are around a million more out there.

Nematodes are quick as lightning and will eat anything in their way; from bacteria, fungi, protozoa, and small insects to decomposing organic matter and other nematodes. The nematodes release plant nutrition once they have processed their food. In particular, they contribute nitrogen, which is beneficial for growing plant roots. Nematodes also create small tunnels for oxygen and water in porous soil. However, the nematodes will move on or die if the soil is compacted, which leads to decreased levels of nitrogen in the soil.

On their way through the porous soil, nematodes happily pick up hitchhikers in the form of bacteria and fungal hyphae, giving these organisms an opportunity to spread quickly.

There are a few harmful nematodes, for example, parasites on plant roots. The soil balance is well maintained in an undisturbed soil, which means the kitchen garden plants won't be bothered by harmful nematodes.

Arthropods, or **invertebrates,** are the largest classification of species on the planet with about 80 percent of all described animals belonging to the group. Most develop in three stages: from egg, to larvae, to adult stage. They are most commonly referred to as insects or crawly critters. The arthropods have different appearances, but all do the same fantastic work breaking up organic matter into smaller pieces, aerating the soil, and creating balance by munching the excess of other soil inhabitants.

Arthropods are divided into four groups:

1. Arachnids. Here we have spiders, pseudoscorpions, opiliones, and mites. All possess superpowers. The hungry moss mites are extremely important as breaker-downers, not least because they are so numerous.
2. Insects. A miscellaneous group of, for example: bees, butterflies, flies, wasps, grasshoppers, springtails, lice, ants, beetles, and dragonflies. It is not only pollinators that are important for cultivation; everybody has a role to play. Springtails are, for example, a delicacy for mites; while the ants chomp down and separate organic matter and turn the soil.
3. Myriapods. We used to call them millipedes but they've now been given more individual precise names like pauropoda, (Hoffman's) dwarf centipede, centipede, and millipedes.

Myriapods work in various ways; the pauropoda eats everything smaller than itself, for example. Meanwhile, the centipede uses toxins in its claws to kill its prey.

4. Crustacean. Most crustaceans are water dwellers. In garden soils, we mostly meet the woodlouse eating primarily dead plant matter, which it excretes to the microorganisms' joy.

The earthworm is often called the gardener's best friend. Nothing strange in that, when you think about the enormous amount of material a single earthworm consumes. It produces 1/30 oz. (1 gr) of humus a day. It might not sound like a lot per worm. However, since good soil can hold up to 500 earthworms per 10¾ sq. ft. (1 m2), calculated at a depth of approximately 10 ft., it is the equivalent of about 1 lb. (500 gr) per 10¾ sq. ft. over 24 hours. Everything from whole plant matter and compost, to bacteria, fungal hyphae, nematodes, protozoa, gravel and stone, is mixed and softened in the worm's tube-like intestine. The material is crushed, pulverized, and processed by enzymes that draw out nutrition before being deposited as super fertilizer. It contains 50 percent more organic material than soil that hasn't passed through an earthworm. The worms also produce mucus that clumps mineral particles and organic materials to units that bind water and nutrition. In its slithering existence, the earthworm moves small stones and soil, simultaneously loosening the soil and creating paths for plant roots, oxygen, and water. As if this wasn't enough, the worm also carries hitchhiking microorganisms along the way. The earthworm is a sensitive creature. It hates compacted or dug-up soils like the plague and dies instantly if the blade of a spade cuts it. However, if the worm is left in peace, it will procreate happily, which means even more nutrient-rich worm excrement.

Gastropods are molluscs with a beautiful house made of lime. They are commonly—and erroneously—called snails. When present in a normal amount, molluscs are useful in the soil where they pulverize and open up organic matter for bacteria and fungal hyphae. They also produce mucus, which binds the soil. The molluscs are also food for other small animals.

THE NUTRITIONAL NETWORK

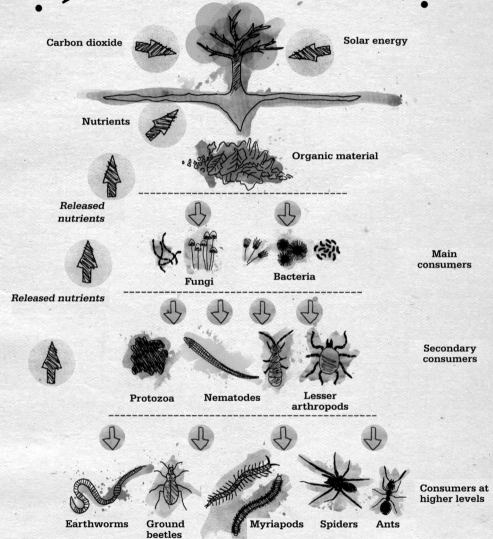

Carbon dioxide

Solar energy

Nutrients

Organic material

Released nutrients

Fungi

Bacteria

Main consumers

Released nutrients

Protozoa

Nematodes

Lesser arthropods

Secondary consumers

Earthworms

Ground beetles

Myriapods

Spiders

Ants

Consumers at higher levels

The nutritional network cycle

The soil organisms need stamina to work and be able to produce nutrition. Most of the energy comes from the sun and is transported down into the soil through the plants. In short, green plants are true energy factories that, through photosynthesis, create food for themselves and others. The plants absorb light, carbon dioxide, and water that are then transformed into carbohydrates. These are used for the plant's metabolism and growth. Oxygen that people and animals breathe is a waste product of this. Ultimately, photosynthesis drives all biological processes on the planet. A healthy soil is, of course, created with mulch material and without digging. Yet it needs photosynthesizing plants during as much of the year as possible.

There is a natural nutritional exchange between microorganisms, soil insects, and plant roots when the soil network remains intact. The nutritional system is balanced in a No-Dig and undisturbed soil; therefore, the inhabitants can give and take in amounts that are good for everyone. The plants get neither more nor less of the nutrients they need, making them healthy and resistant to diseases and pests in the long run.

When mulch and compost are added to the soil, both the level of organic material and the microbial variety increases. If the soil is also left in peace, the plants will grow healthily instead of stressed. The plants get the strength to build vegetation and roots through photosynthesis. In addition, they dish out sugar, starch, and protein to the organisms in the soil. Once the microorganisms have eaten their fill and done their work, in a nifty cycle, they'll return nutrition to the plant in a new form.

THE NUTRITIONAL CYCLE—THIS IS HOW IT WORKS

1) Bacteria and fungal hyphae congregate close to the plant roots and receive sugar, starch, and protein secreted from the root hairs. This gives the microorganisms the strength to separate nutrients from the matter in the soil, thrive, and reproduce.

2) Protozoans, nematodes, and smaller arthropods are attracted to nutrient-rich bacteria and fungal hyphae, swallowing them lock, stock, and barrel. A balance is soon reached between the numbers of members from the two working groups. When the secondary consumers leave a surplus comparable to excreta, or die and decompose, all the nutrients from bacteria and fungal hyphae become available to the plant roots.

3) Now the larger arthropods (i.e. all our planet's insects and creepy crawlies) turn up and gulp down protozoans and nematodes. They also attack organic matter, dividing it into smaller pieces that bacteria and fungi then break down to mold.

Mycorrhiza—a vital network

Of all the life in the soil perhaps the most important is the symbiosis between plant roots and the specific mycorrhiza fungi. The fungi attach themselves directly against the plant roots and quickly create an extensive network of hyphae that search out nutrients in every nook and cranny where the roots otherwise can't reach. Thanks to enzymes in the fungi, the hyphae can even eat through stone, collecting mineral elements like phosphorus, nitrogen, sulfur, and calcium. However, the mycorrhiza doesn't give the plant roots something for nothing. Payment is made with carbohydrates from the plant's photosynthesis.

The mycorrhiza network works, in principle, like an increased root system. Garden plants with small roots, like onions and leeks, grow so much better if they get a helping hand with the nutrient uptake. Digging doesn't just cause an upheaval in the ground; the spade also breaks apart the hyphae that are meant to deliver nutrients to your plants.

Unfortunately, it isn't only the spade that renders the mycorrhiza unusable. The fungi need host plants to survive. Otherwise, they'll disappear in areas they don't find teammates. For example, the mycorrhiza will not connect with the cruciferous family (which includes a variety of cabbages). If you grow cabbages in the same area for a long time, the mycorrhiza and the magical network will fade away. This is a very compelling reason for practicing crop rotations as well as growing a wide variety of plants in the garden beds.

Cabbage stems with roots left in the ground.

The importance of pH

The soil pH level (i.e. acidity) influences nutrient availability for the plants. The pH value is graded on a scale of 1 to 14, where 7 is neutral. A low pH level shows an acidic soil, while a higher level shows an alkaline soil.

It was once believed that kitchen garden plants thrive best in

MYCORRHIZA

neutral soil. Nowadays, it's understood they want a slightly more acidic soil.

A pH level around 6 makes most nutrients available to the plants. Using lime in the soil to neutralize or make acidic soil more alkaline used to be a common practice. Today we know it's more likely to block the uptake of elements like iron, manganese, boron, zinc, copper, magnesium, and nickel, at the same time making phosphorus less available to the plants.

A No-Dig garden bed that is mulched or covered with compost keeps a balanced pH level thanks to the busy microorganisms processing organic materials. A large number of worms is a sign the soil is maintaining a good pH level. Worms thrive in a pH level around 6–6.5, which also means soil full of worms is also perfect plant soil. You can buy a pH meter in the plant nursery if you're unsure about your soil's balance.

GEOLOGY

Cultivation is about making sure the soil is healthy so it can provide growing plants with a good, nourishing environment. In other words, you're cultivating the soil more than specific plants.

By getting to know the soil and its construction it is easier to understand why your plantings behave the way they do.

This is the soil's physical structure

Soil can be built in two ways: first, from mineral grains from the bedrock; and second, from organic matter that falls on the ground, which the microorganisms then convert into soil. Helped by glue-like mucus from the soil's microorganisms, the mineral particles clump together into small grainy units, binding both water and nutrients. The units are invaluable in another way. Small holes, or pores, form between the units, through which oxygen and moisture can stream and plant roots can wander deeper down to collect water and nutrition. A soil with good structure has an even network of pores and retains water as well as a sponge.

Soil types are defined by the mineral particles that have chafed, crumbled, or broken out of bedrock through natural chemical processes. The size of the grain decides soil type; the smaller the grain the larger the total area that can store nutrition. The bedrock itself also determines how nutritious the soil will become. For example, lime-rich bedrock is very rich in nutrients while quartz-rich bedrock is less so. There are also organic varieties like mud, silt, and peat that are created from incomplete moldered plant matter and animal carcasses in damp and oxygen-poor environments. You won't find peat moss and mud in gardens for the simple reason that neither is suitable for building habitation nor creating gardens on. Four common kinds of soil are sand, silt, clay, and moraine.

- **Sand** has large grains, making it porous and early to warm up in spring. It doesn't clump, and therefore it's bad at retaining nutrients and moisture. By adding a large amount of organic matter, sand can be amended into fine garden soil. Sand is divided into coarse, medium, and fine-grained.

- **Silt** has smaller grains than sand and has unstable units; the particles easily come loose from each other and float away in water. Silt is good at retaining moisture and nutrients but can be smashed up by heavy rain or working the soil, leading to crust formation and, in the long run, flooding with heavy rains. No-Dig gardening is the perfect method for silt soil, which gratefully receives compost or mulching materials for protection. Silt is divided into coarse, medium, and fine silt.

- **Clay soil** is composed of loads of tiny particles that easily clump into units. It is very fertile and moisture-retaining because every little particle binds nutrients and moisture. The combined area is huge. Because of its moisture-retaining ability, clay soil doesn't warm up until late in the spring. Soil with high clay content is also dense, has difficulty breathing, and is very sensitive to compacting and processing. Clay soil is made for No-Dig gardening; as long as it's amended on the surface with organic material and left in peace it will offer wonderful gardening soil. Soil is classified as clay when it contains 5 percent clay particles. At 15 percent it's called light clay, and the classification increases from there. At percentages higher than 40 percent it's referred to as fat clay.

- **Moraine soil** is a mixture of everything from fine clay particles to stones. Depending on the size of particles, there exists everything from stony and poor to fat and nutrient-rich moraine soils. A moraine soil with a high clay content is called moraine clay and is great soil for cultivation.

Soil is the ground's top layer and is made of materials typical for the area. Microorganisms, together with water and heat, converted the materials. Different areas have different kinds of soil depending on mineral grain size and type of vegetation, microorganisms, the water content, and climate.

- **Podzol** is meager and nutrient-poor. It's usually present in coniferous woods.
- **Brown earth** is nutrient-rich and well drained with neutral pH. Brown soil has two layers. Resting against the bedrock is pan (or "hardpan"), which is basically bedrock undergoing the process of breaking down. On top is a layer of mineral soil mixed with organic matter in various stages of decomposition.

Humus or **mold** is the processed organic matter that originated from plant and animal parts, along with all the microorganisms binding nutrition and circulating in the living nutritional network. It's a continuous process of living material mixing with dead matter in a constant flux.

Humus is a dark-colored, soil-like substance in which the original individual materials are not recognizable. Mold contributes structure and warmth and also retains nutrients and moisture. A soil rich in mold survives periods of drought and heavy rains. Mold is not nourishing in itself but has the ability to bind nutrients, preventing nutrition from leaching out. Instead, the nutrition is released continually throughout the season, making it available when the plants need it. Humus binds carbon and nitrogen.

WEIGHT

The mold level refers to how much of the soil has organic origin. An ideal garden soil has a 10 percent mold level. This is composed of about half mineral soil and half decomposed plant debris. The mold level is calculated by percent of the weight, the mineral particles being heavier per volume than organic matter. To keep the soil rich in mold you'll need to continually feed it with new organic matter because it's constantly being broken down.

GET TO KNOW THE SOIL

You'll learn plenty about your soil by handling it with your hands:

Level of mold: Take a handful of dirt and press it together lightly. The mold level is high if it's light brown, keeps the shape easily, and feels like a sponge that lets only a few drops of water through.

Soil type. Take a handful of dirt and roll it between your hands. What you feel leads to these conclusions:

• The dirt is grainy and falls apart = sandy soil.
• The dirt feels grainy but doesn't crumble = sand mixed with clay.
• The dirt doesn't feel grainy and doesn't stick to the fingers = slight clay.
• The dirt is sticky and has a smooth shiny surface when pressed on = fat or light clay.
• The surface is neither smooth nor shiny = moraine with clay.

Topsoil/garden soil is the layer which people cultivate, dress with manure and organic matter, and then garden in. The quality of the topsoil depends on the kind of earth and soil and also on humus level. However, the quality benefits primarily when microbial life can work undisturbed with the organic materials placed on the surface. A good topsoil/garden soil is dark brown, porous, smells nice, and retains water.

VEGETABLE FAVORITES

Everything grown using traditional methods can also be grown in No-Dig gardening beds, where both annuals and perennials have a tendency to thrive. Instead of using your time and energy digging, watering, and fertilizing, use it to select seeds and plants. The challenge will be figuring out which plants do well in companion plantings, the space requirements required for each, and which ones are suitable for succession plantings in order to provide continuous and extended harvests.

ANNUALS—FOR BIG AND DEPENDABLE CROPS

Here are some annuals (grown for only one year), which yield large and tasty crops. Don't forget to grow several different varieties; it's nice to have some diversity.

Legumes

Beans, lentils, and **peas** are legumes belonging to the *Fabaceae* family. Legumes are named for the pod (the capsule-like fruit) that holds their seeds. Legumes are perfect for the No-Dig beds because they contribute nitrogen they get from the air, transporting it down into the soil. They leave behind plenty of mulching materials once the crop is harvested. Legumes can also stand close in a No-Dig bed, which results in large yields.

Two good options include the common/French bean, *Phaseolus vulgaris,* and common garden peas, *Pisum sativum.* You'll find both low- and tall-growing varieties and the pods have different shapes and colors. It's smart to go with tall-growing peas and beans to ensure large crops. Supply them with sturdy supports for climbing so they don't collapse and die on the ground.

Legumes grow quickly, so they don't need to be started indoors. However, it's not a bad idea to start some in order to harvest a crop earlier. In the northern United States, seed-starting indoors is more or less a prerequisite to get a harvest before the season is over. Planting early varieties also helps. Start the pre-cultivation a few weeks before the plants are placed out in your garden so they don't grow too big or are forced to fight for space in the pots.

Both beans and peas are pure kitchen garden treasures. They yield a lot of food in a small space, are loaded with proteins, minerals, and vitamins, and provide the soil with nutrients for the next season. And, the more pods you pick the more pods they produce.

Broad/fava bean, *Vicia faba,* is a delicious treat with a nutty flavor. It's probably at its best eaten newly picked, lightly blanched, and tossed in butter. It can also be frozen or dried for winter storage. The frost-tolerant broad/fava bean is a fine legume. Well, it isn't a legume, really. The broadbean belongs to the vetch family, *Vicia Faba.*

The broad bean grows into a 3¼ ft. (100 cm) -tall bush and can be directly sown early, when soil temperatures are between 39.2°F–41°F (4°C–5°C). Broad beans are also suitable for pre-cultivation, having plants ready to set out at the start of the growing season. The beans can be grown in clusters. They will then support each other and yield a large crop in a small area. To prevent the plants from bowing, tie the clusters together with twine.

Common garden bean, *Phaseolus vulgaris,* produces a lot of food and has many varieties. They are divided into five groups:

Sugar pea

Haricots verts, yellow wax bean, purple bean, kidney bean, and common green bean. Each group has low- and tall-growing varieties. Bush beans are low growing, around 1 ft. (40 cm) tall. Tall growing or pole beans can reach 6½ ft. (200 cm) or more and need trellises to climb. The tall-growing varieties give the highest crop yield. The garden bean is directly sown in warm soil that needs to reach at least 53°F (12°C). They are excellent for pre-cultivation to have plants on hand once the soil temperature is right or to fill in empty spaces in a garden bed. Erecting a trellis when sowing the seeds will make it easy to guide the plants while they grow. This is how you identify the different garden beans:

- Snap beans, also called Haricots verts, have long cylinder-shaped green pods that are eaten whole.
- Yellow wax beans are the same shape as the Haricots verts but have yellow pods and are eaten whole.
- Purple beans are the same shape as the Haricots verts but purple and are eaten whole.
- Flat or Romano beans have wide, flat pods in green, yellow, or lilac colors. Usually eaten cut up.
- Broad beans are grown for the beans. The pods are opened and emptied out.

Peas, *Pisum sativum,* are deliciously sweet and fun to grow and eat. They are divided into several groups: usually sugar peas, sugar snap peas, marrow peas, shelling round peas, and dried shelling peas. Peas are grouped by the appearance of pods and peas, how they are used, by height, and how early they are. Garden peas vary in height, from 10 in. (25 cm) bush varieties, to tall varieties that can reach more than 6½ ft. (200 cm) and need to be supported. Sugar and shelling peas can be sown when the soil is at only 41°F (5°C). Marrow and sugar snap peas need warmer soil or they risk rotting if the soil temperature is below 50°F (10°C). Here are the different pea characteristics:

- Sugar peas develop flat, crisp pods that are harvested before the peas inside have developed. There are green, yellow, and lilac. The peas are eaten raw or cooked.

- Snap, or sugar snap peas, are commercially bred and a slightly meatier version of the sugar pea. They produce sweet green tasty pods that are eaten raw or cooked.
- Shelling peas, usually just called green peas, are grown for the peas themselves and are shucked before use. The peas are round, smooth, and somewhat floury. They are eaten raw or cooked.
- Marrow pea, a kind of shelling pea, is shucked from the pods. The peas are dented and often taste slightly sweet. They are eaten raw or cooked.
- Cooked shelling peas. These are the dried seeds of shelling peas. The peas are dried for storage and need to be soaked before cooking. The grey field pea is an old, protein-rich version of the shelling pea and its popularity is growing.

SUPPORTS FOR LEGUMES

Tall legume plants need sturdy support like poles with climb-friendly chicken fencing or string lines stretched between them.

Bush varieties might need some support. Cut off a few 1½ ft.–3¼ ft. (50 cm–100 cm) sturdy twigs and push them into the soil along the plant row.

Broad beans get good support by a pole in each corner of the planting area and a string encircling the plants.

Legumes—first-rate varieties

Broad/Fava bean "Express" is a lower-growing, early, and fruitful plant with 6 in. (15 cm) pods.

Haricots verts "Cobra" is a tall-growing and more delicate haricots verts variety that is good to freeze.

Purple pole bean "Blauhilde" grows tall, is relatively early, and produces 6–8 in. (15 cm–20 cm) purple pods that turn green when cooked.

Kidney pole bean "Eva," a tall-growing, fast producer that makes juicy and delicate green flat round pods.

Wax pole bean "Neckargold" produces sturdy and round yellow tasty pods of good quality. Slightly later in the season and has 10 in. (25 cm) pods.

Shelling bean "Lingua di Fuoco Nano" is a tall-growing borlotto bean with mottled pods and wine-red patterned whitish-yellow seeds. These are blanched and eaten fresh or are dried for winter storage.

POLLINATION HELP

Many summer squashes have only female flowers and are self-fertile (i.e. they don't depend on pollinators). Others, both squash and pumpkins, have big yellow flowers of both sexes on the same plant. Usually several male flowers appear first. The female flower develops when it gets really warm. They have a small swollen embryonic organ at the base that develops into a fruit if pollinated. If there is a lack of bumblebees and honeybees in the garden you might have to help the flowers along with the pollination. Carefully rub a male flower against the female flower pistil or brush between the flowers with a soft brush.

Sugar pea "Norli" is a productive variety with long, fresh, sweet and tasty pods that develop fast. The plant grows to about 2 ft. (60 cm).

Sugar Snap pea "Sugar Ann" is an extra early bush variety with lots of sweet, delicate, and chubby pods. Fast and dependable.

Marrow pea "Alderman" is a tall marrow pea variety that yields generous crops of 4½–5 in. (11–13 cm) straight pods with large, sweet peas.

Shelling pea "Meteor" is low growing, cold-hardy, and early. Produces large harvests of dark green, 2¾ in. (7 cm) pods with round, mealy peas.

Fruiting vegetables

Pumpkin and **squash** belong to the cucumber family, *Cucurbitaceae*. They are very simple to grow, are great producers, and they offer edible flowers. Both squash and pumpkins want warm, nutrient-rich soil—they need it to be at least 59°F (15°C) to grow. They can be directly sown in hardiness zones of 3 or above, which is all of the United States. If you do need to start them indoors, remember that the plants grow quickly so it is unnecessary to sow them too early. It takes four weeks from seeding to setting out. Sensitive to frost, they should not be set out in the garden before the last frosty nights are well past.

One or two plants of each variety is usually enough, but there are so many fun ones it's difficult to choose. The plants occupy a lot of space, which could be a problem. On the other hand, the long stems spread over the bed like a living mulch cover, providing a great environment for beans and peas that grow upright.

There's some confusion around what's what when we talk about pumpkin and squash; originally from the same family, they are sorted by appearance, harvest time, and storage properties.

Summer squash "Costata Romanesco"

Winter squash "Uchiki Kuri"

Cucurbita pepo is the most common and the easiest to grow. This kind includes varieties with thin peel and white flesh, and is often called summer squash or zucchini. It's harvested during the summer and is very perishable, so it can't be stored for any length of time. We include the so-called pie pumpkins; the big round kind which have harder skin and flesh, and as a result, can be stored. These plants are bush-like. A few varieties have winding stems and tendrils.

Cucurbita maxima is another common variety. It includes a lot of common food pumpkins, which we also call winter squashes. The fruits ripen during late summer and fall, vary a lot in shape and coloration, and have hard skin with firm flesh. These can be stored for long periods and some growers display them as artwork on shelves in their homes. The plants grow long stems and tendrils.

Cucurbita moschata include musk pumpkin and butternut. They are peanut-shaped fruits with firm flesh and a sweet, nutty flavor.

Pumpkin and squash—first-rate varieties

"Costata Romanesco" is the most flavorful summer squash there is. The plant is bush-like with sturdy leaves. The fruits get light ridges over a pale green background. The male flowers are big and great for frying or deep-frying.

"Cocozelle" is a bush squash with long cylinder-shaped fruits. The skin is light green with dark green stripes. The flesh is light and firm with good flavor.

"Tondo Chiaro di Nizza" produces very flavorful round globe fruits. Thin skin with light dots.

"Yellow crookneck" is an heirloom squash from the 18th century. Grows like a bush with up to 6½ ft. (200 cm) stems and tendrils. The fruits are small, yellow, and bowling pin-shaped with a bent neck. Firm flesh with a buttery flavor.

"Blue Hubbard" is a large pumpkin with orange, rich, sweet-tasting flesh. It grows quickly and puts out long stems and produces dome-like, hard fruits with nearly silver-blue skin. May weigh between 4½–33 lb. (2 kg–15 kg) and can be stored for up to one year.

"Kroschka" produces light grey 4½ lb. (2 kg) pumpkins with sweet, orange-colored flesh. It puts out long stems with tendrils with 2 to 3 fruits per plant. Reliable and fruits mature even during lousy summers. The fruits keep well for one year.

"Uchiki Kuri" is a sturdy-growing winter squash with drop-shaped orange-red 4½ lb. (2 kg) fruits. Fiberless flesh with a nutty flavor. Stores well if harvested late.

"Sweet Dumpling" is a winter squash that produces 10½ oz. (300 gr) creamy-white, flat round fruits with dark green ribs. Butter-yellow flesh with a smooth, sweet flavor. Winding 6½ ft. (2 m) stems. Stores well for three to four months.

"Early butternut" is a musk pumpkin that matures early in the season. Big with long stems, it produces up to four 4½ lb. (2 kg) fruits per plant. Longish fruits with a nutty flavor.

Tomatoes, *Solanum lycopersicum*; there are thousands of varieties, all in different colors, shapes, flavors, and with different storage possibilities. Few vegetables give so many and such exciting harvests. If that's not enough, the season is long. With good planning you can eat fresh tomatoes from the beginning of June until Christmas. The so-called winter tomatoes are fantastic and they can be kept fresh far into winter. Pick complete branches with tomatoes and hang them upside down in the kitchen. Tomatoes can also be put up, made into tomato sauce, preserved, or frozen whole.

Tomato plants are usually divided into two groups: indeterminate and determinate. A determinate tomato plant will stop growing after the fruit sets on the top bud. Indeterminate plants continue growing and producing flowers.

In most growing zones, tomatoes have to be started indoors to develop in time to produce a crop. Check online to see when to start tomatoes in your zone. Transplant seedlings outside in a sunny and protected area.

Siberian varieties are truly tough customers as they can grow and set fruit in only 50°–59°F (10°C–15°C), which is perfect for outdoor gardening in high altitudes. Indeterminate tomato plants will sprout suckers in the joints between stem and leaf. These should be pinched off so they don't steal the energy needed to produce tomatoes. Indeterminate tomato plants need to be supported. Determinate tomatoes, a.k.a. "bush" tomatoes, are easier to handle, as they need neither support nor pinching.

STRING AROUND THE ROOT

Place a string around the bottom of the plant when planting an indeterminate tomato plant. When time comes to bind it up for support, the string is already there and you don't have to bother with knots around the stem.

There are thousands of tomato varieties, in all different colors, shapes, and flavors.

SUNNY GREETINGS TO TOMATO GROWERS

• You can remove leaves up to at least the first fruits once the plant has stopped growing. That way the sun will reach the ripening tomatoes.
• It is important to ventilate properly if you grow in a greenhouse. The pollen quality is degraded if it gets too hot, which results in fewer tomatoes.

GIVE THE PLANT A SHAKE TO HELP WITH POLLINATION

The tomato plant is self-fertile—its pollen doesn't need to move from flower to flower for pollination. All the same, the plant needs a light shake to aid the pollen grains in landing in the right place. Give the plant a light shake daily during flowering. Do this preferably in the early morning—it is said that the pollen lets go before 11 a.m.

Tomatoes—first-rate varieties

"Brandywine" is a beefsteak heirloom variety from 1885. Usually produces oblate, nearly pink full-flavored fruits. It exists in several color variations and flavors. Brandywine has unusual "potato" leaves (round with pointy tips) and grows 6½ ft. (200 cm) tall; the plant needs to be supported and to have suckers pinched off. Brandywine is grown in a warm protected area or in a greenhouse.

"Principe Borghese" is a winter tomato, sometimes called "eternal tomato," that keeps for a long time. Produces oval, 1½–2 in. (4 cm–5 cm) fruits with a point at the end. The plant grows about 6½ ft. (200 cm) and needs to be bound up for support and have suckers pinched off. A hardy tomato for outside. Pruned branches with tomatoes can be strung up with looped rope from the ceiling, a storage method called *piennolo*. The tomatoes dry somewhat during storage, which gives them a wonderfully concentrated flavor.

"Indigo Rose" is a purplish-black tomato that develops a deep red color and plum-like flavor when mature. The skin is a bit coarser and it matures late, which makes it suitable for storage. It is grown in a warm outdoor location or in a greenhouse. Plants grow to 6½ ft. (200 cm) and need support and to have suckers pinched.

"Koralik" is a determinate (bush-like growth) tomato that produces lots of lipstick red cherry tomatoes. Grows sturdily and wide but generally only reaches 8–10 in. (20 cm–25 cm) high (though some varieties grow up to 4' tall), which makes it easy to grow in a container. Does very well outdoors.

"Sibirjak" is a fast-growing, hardy bush tomato that doesn't mind a cooler climate, doing very well outdoors. Produces large, tasty fruits. The plant reaches about 3¼ ft. (1 m) and needs support and also to have suckers pinched off.

"Sungold" F1 is an early cherry tomato and one of the sweetest there is, with juicy, golden orange fruits. It is grown outdoors in a warm location or in a greenhouse. The plant grows to 5 ft. (150 cm) and needs support and to have suckers removed.

Root vegetables

Potatoes, *Solanum tuberosum,* give variety, satiety, and vitamins and are easy to grow, to boot. They are also excellent to use as a first crop when you're breaking in a new garden bed because the roots work and loosen the soil naturally.

Potatoes are reproduced by planting seed potatoes you have either grown yourself and put away for next year, or with certified potatoes from the plant nursery. Certified potatoes are checked to ensure they are not carriers of too high levels of diseases like virus, rot, and scab. The perfect seed potato is 2 in. (5 cm) in diameter. Plant the potatoes when the ground is 46.4°F (8°C).

If exposed to light, the growing potato bumps will turn green and toxic, so you have to shade them (i.e. cover or "hill") with soil as they grow. The mulch protects them from light in a mulched bed. In a composted bed you will have to hill the compost around the plant as it grows.

Don't grow potatoes in pure cow compost. All the nutrition in the compost stresses the plant to grow too quickly and take over, and the potatoes risk being affected by scab.

PRE-SPROUTING (CHITTING) FOR EARLY AND PREDICTABLE CROP

Pre-sprouting of the potatoes shortens time spent in the bed, which produces an early and often bigger crop. It's also a way to avoid potato leaf mold that arrives later in the season. Thus you'll have time to harvest the potatoes before the disease attacks.

How to pre-sprout:

Start four to five weeks before you want to plant. Keep the potatoes in a warm and dark location for a few days, and then remove them to a light 50°F–59°F (10°C–15°C), warm room. Place the potatoes in containers where they will develop sprouts, which at planting time should be chubby and around ½ in. (1 cm) long. If the potatoes are placed on a bed of damp compost or soil, both sprouts and roots will develop, giving an even better growing advantage. It is time to plant the potatoes once the garden soil has reached 46.4°F (8°C).

Potatoes—first-rate varieties

"Casablanca" is a very early, abundant, and tasty variety. Firm, white flesh and oval shape.

"Rocket" is a very early variety. Firm flesh. Round, white, and fast growing. Resistant to potato wart and nematodes. Suitable for boiling, frying, and roasting.

"Amandine" is another early potato. Firm. Elongated shape and pale

Potatoes are easy to harvest
with a pitchfork.

yellow flesh with perfect texture and gourmet flavor. Resistant to potato wart and scab.

"Provita" is an early variety. Somewhat mealy. Produces smooth, oval potatoes with pale yellow flesh. Can be left for a long time in the ground without growing too much. Stores very well. Is resistant against potato wart and nematodes and has some resistance against potato leaf mold.

"Allians" is a late variety. Firm. Produces a large crop of oval potatoes with thin skin, yellow flesh, and buttery flavor. Resistant to potato wart, nematodes, and potato leaf mold.

"Asterix" is a late variety. Somewhat mealy texture. Produces red-skinned, oval potatoes with good flavor; a generous producer and good for cooking. Resistant to potato wart and nematodes. Has some resistance to potato leaf mold.

"Ovatio" is a late variety. Floury. Large crops of big, oval potatoes with good flavor. Resistant to potato wart and nematodes. Some resistance to potato leaf mold.

"Sarpo Mira" is another late variety. Floury. Easy to grow and high-yielding. Produces roundish oval potatoes with pink skin and pale yellow flesh. Resistant to potato leaf mold. Resistant to potato wart but less resistant to nematodes.

POTATO SMARTS

• You don't have to throw away potatoes that have turned green and toxic. Save and use them as seed potatoes next year.

• A large seed potato will produce lots of small potatoes, while small seed potatoes produce larger potatoes. Large seed potatoes can be halved. Make sure each piece has eyes that can sprout. Let the cut surface dry out before you plant the pieces.

Carrots, *Daucus carota* ssp. *sativus*, exist in lots of colors and shapes and are highly nutritious. They are very suitable for succession planting in No-Dig garden beds.

Variety-wise, you'll find fast-growing summer carrots for early harvests and succession planting, and then sturdy fall and winter varieties that will be fine to store. Summer varieties take about three months to maturation, fall and winter varieties demand four to five months before they are ready to be harvested. Carrots are tricky to start indoors because some roots are always damaged when planted out, making the root branch. To get multiple harvests, succession plant several times during the season. In some areas, carrots can be sown as often as twice in the spring—the first time when the soil has reached 50°F (10°C), then at the end of June—and several times in November. The seeds overwinter in the ground after fall sowing, ready to start growing early in the spring. Carrots are biennial plants but are harvested as annuals. You'll only save some plants for the next year if you collect the seeds.

Early carrot varieties risk splitting if they stay in the soil longer than three weeks after they're harvest ready. Fall and winter carrots grow best in the fall and should be harvested as late in the season as possible if you want to store them.

Carrots—first-rate varieties

"Amsterdam Forcing" is a delicate and sweet summer carrot with a thin core. The color is a nice orange; the roots are cylindrical and grow to 4½–5 in. (11 cm–13 cm).

"Purple Haze" F1 has a purple red exterior with an orange core. This is a summer carrot that grows 7–8 in. (18 cm–20 cm) conical roots. Delicate and sweet.

"Paris Market" is a fast-growing globe-shaped summer carrot with a sweet flavor. Its short shape, 1¼–2 in. (3 cm–5 cm), makes it suitable even for fat clay soils and shallower grow boxes.

"Early Nantes" is an early and dependable variety with delicate, cylindrical roots and nice orange color. Perfect to eat fresh but can stay in the soil during an extended period without splitting.

"White Satin" is a summer carrot with white, 8–10 in. (20 cm–25 cm) conical roots. Mild and sweet flavor.

FAMILY FEUD

Don't grow dill and carrots together. They are close relatives but dislike each other intensely.

KEEP RESEEDING!

Early carrots are fast growers and great for succession planting even in late summer. Sow them, for example, as a second crop after early potatoes or garlic.

"London Torg" is a fall carrot that grows short in length but is "wide-shouldered." Red-orange with a nice-tasting juicy root. Great for storing.

"Yellowstone" is a smooth and evenly cone-shaped yellow fall carrot with tasty, delicate flesh. Good for storing.

"Autumn King" is a good and dependable, strong-growing fall and winter carrot with somewhat cone-shaped roots and thin core. Good for eating fresh but can also be stored for extended periods.

"Rothild" is a juicy fall and winter carrot with high levels of beta-carotene. It has an excellent flavor and strong color. Big, slightly cone-shaped root, 8–10 in. (20 cm–25 cm) long. Stores well.

"Jaune du Doubs" is a yellow winter carrot. Mild and round carrot flavor, delicate when young and full-flavored as mature carrot.

Crisp carrots, mixed varieties

Celeriac "Printz"

Parsnip, *Pastinaca sativa,* is easy to grow and does great in a No-Dig garden bed. It is a slow-growing rascal that takes its time. It's well worth the wait as it is fiber-, vitamin-, and mineral-rich. Let's not forget, it has fantastic flavor too. Parsnips can be directly sown early in the spring but preferably in the fall before the frost hits, letting the seed rest in the soil to wait for spring. Mark the rows clearly so any necessary weeding in spring can be accomplished without damaging the young plants. Parsnips can't be pre-cultivated indoors as the fragile root threads are easily damaged when planted out, and the root branches as a result. Parsnips can be grown in clusters, but will then produce slightly smaller roots. Remember that parsnips taste best after a nip of frost so wait to harvest as long as possible.

Parsnips—first-rate varieties

"White Gem" is the most frequently grown parsnip. The root is average in length with smooth, white skin and tasty flesh. Has good resistance against brown (leaf) rust and scab. Can be stored.
"Student" is an old and dependable variety with even cone-shaped roots and nice flavor. Very resistant to scab. Can be stored.
"Halblange Weiss" is an early variety with creamy yellow, even cone-shaped roots. It is mostly grown for fall and winter crops but is also good as mini parsnip earlier in the season. Hardy and can overwinter.

Celeriac, *Apium graveolens,* is a nutritious and flavorful root vegetable that is often used as a main ingredient in vegetarian dishes. Celeriac is a slow grower and needs to be sown indoors 10 to 12 weeks before transplanting outdoors. Celeriac needs to be potted up at least once to develop properly, and then be transplanted outside when the ground has warmed up and all threat of night frost is past. Young celeriac root is sensitive to quick temperature changes. If exposed to cold it might start early flowering, also known as bolting. Apart from that, it will grow meaty and fine in No-Dig garden soil. When mature, it can weather some below freezing temperatures. You will need a fork hand-tool to loosen the soil at harvest because the celeriac clings to the soil for dear life.

Celeriac—first-rate varieties

"Monarch" is a healthy, hardy celeriac with good storage capacity. High-domed, round and heavy with white, firm flesh and mild, nutty flavor.

"Mars," also high-domed, with fine quality white flesh. Grows well in clay soil and produces a large and storage-suitable fall crop.

"Printz" is fast-growing and produces small to average, somewhat flat, round bulbs. The flesh is white, flavorful, crisp and firm. Good for storage.

Beets, *Beta vulgaris,* mostly mean red for us. However, they have siblings that are everything from yellow and white, to striped red/white. It is easier to call the whole group just "beets." Beets are a quick crop, they only need two months from seed to harvest, and are suitable for succession planting. Directly sow beets when the soil has reached 46.4°F (8°C). They can also be started indoors to have transplants ready when gaps open up in beds after harvests. Beets thrive in the porous No-Dig garden beds. Thinning out the small plants to create space for growth results in even-sized beets that can be harvested together. The thinned-out leaves are great for salads. Beets can also grow in clusters where they kind of climb on each other, pushing each other over into more growing space. Every seed makes several plants so clusters will happen naturally if you don't thin out the growing plants.*

Beets—first-rate varieties

"Boltardy" is perfect for early planting as they don't bolt. The beets are round, dark red with a diameter of up to 4 in. (10 cm). The flesh is crisp and sweet. Good for storage.

"Detroit 2" is globe-shaped with thin, smooth skin and deep red flesh throughout. Low nitrate level. This one is suitable for early sowing and harvest as well as for fall harvest and storage.

"Cylindra" is a cylinder-shaped beet with a 6–7 in. (15 cm–18 cm) root, thin skin, and reddish violet flesh with sweet balanced flavor. Good eaten fresh and for preserving and storing.

"Blankorna" is a globe-shaped, white beet with a mild and sweet flavor. It needs to be soil covered (hilled) to not get a green neck. Good for storing.

*Some beet seeds are monoembryonic, while many are polyembryonic.

Beets grow very well in
No-Dig garden beds.

Onions need to be air-dried before storing.

"Detroit Golden Beet" is a sweet, fine, and reliable yellow beet crop. Produces evenly shaped, somewhat elongated beets.

"Chioggia" is a stripy beet where the white flesh has rose red rings. Globe-shaped root with sweet flavor. Keeps well in long storage.

Onion, *Allium cepa,* is easy to grow, adds that umami flavor to most dishes, contains Vitamin C, and helps to lower cholesterol and stabilize blood glucose levels. A great plant that thrives in No-Dig garden beds. The most common way to grow is to plant nursery-cultivated onion sets. Today you can buy heat-treated onions, which reduces the risk for early flowering/bolting. The variety in onion sets is limited, so if you want more to choose from you will have to start them from seed. Depending on where you live, you may need to start seeds in February–March to get them ready in time. Sow them in clusters of four to six seeds in each pot/cell, pot them up into a larger pot when it starts to look crowded, and plant them in the garden bed when the risk for frost is past.

Leeks, *Allium porrum,* also have to be started indoors, preferably growing them in clusters.

There are several varieties of edible onions:

Yellow and **red onion,** *Allium cepa,* is the most common culinary onion. Both grow to 1–4 in. (3 cm–10 cm) in diameter. Red onion has a slightly milder flavor than yellow.

Frying/roasting onion is a smaller version of yellow and red onion. The diameter is less than 1½ in. (3⅕ cm). The flavor is the same as for the larger onion. Suitable for roasting whole.

Pearl onion is a close relative of the common yellow onion. It often has a somewhat flat, round shape, and measures about 1–2 in. (3 cm–5 cm) in diameter. Mild flavor.

Shallots are nearly drop-shaped *cepa* onions. There are often two cloves inside the tunic (outer layer), and they are round and mild tasting. Shallots grow in bunches of 4 to 8 small onions around each onion set.

White globe onions have a silvery outer layer and pure white interior. They are milder than red and yellow *cepa* onions and are eaten fresh, as they don't store at all.

Leeks contain twice (2x) as much fiber as other onions and much more Vitamin C. They can be used raw or cooked in all food preparation. Leeks grow late into fall, tolerate a frosty night, and produce more the longer they're left in the garden bed.

EXCITING ONION VARIETIES

Walking onion/tree onion, *Allium x proliferum,* develops onion clusters at the top of the stalks and underground. It's perennial and very hardy. Used as a salad onion, chives, and for cooking.

Welsh onion/bunching onion/spring onion, *Allium fistulosum,* grows in clumps and produces strong, hollow stems that are used like chives or leeks. Perennial.

Potato onions/hill onions, *Allium cepa* var. *aggregatum,* grows clusters of small onions underground and is regarded as the shallot's poorer relative. Good culinary onion. Hardy and can be grown in zones as cold as USDA Zone 4.

Ramson, *Allium ursinum,* is a perennial grove plant that grows wide, lancet-like leaves and stalks with star-like flowers. Grows naturally in lime-rich soils. It is primarily the young leaves that are used. They are used as chives, in soups and pesto, in pickling, and dried in salt mixes. The seed capsules can be made into ramson capers.

Onions—first-rate varieties

"Sturon" is an heirloom yellow onion with juicy flesh. Resistant to bolting. Great for storing.

"Ailsa Craig" is a very large yellow onion with a sweet and mild flavor. Good to store for a few months.

"Red Baron" is round to oblate, dark red, with a mild and sweet flavor. Slightly late variety with narrow neck and strong outer peel. Good for storing.

"Golden Gourmet" is a shallot with a delicate aromatic flavor. Can be stored; dry it hanging for best result.

"Snowball" is a white globe onion with a mild, slightly spicy flavor. Suitable for eating raw but not for storage.

"Atal" is an early leek for eating fresh. Produces tender, light green stalk on a long white base. It's harvested in late summer.

"Musselburgh" is a sturdy thick-necked fall leek with white stalks and a good mild flavor. Perfect for the Nordic climate. Very cold hardy.

Garlic, *Allium sativum,* is a much-appreciated culinary ingredient. It also has some antibacterial properties thanks to the compound allicin. Garlic is divided into *hardnecks* and *softnecks.* Hardneck has a stiff stem and superior flavor, but it can't be braided nor does it store well. Softneck can be braided and it stores well—it's great to always have a braid handy in the kitchen.

Garlic is planted in fall to give the onion time to root before the ground frost hits, but it doesn't start growing before winter.

Garlic is planted in late fall and gives summer harvest.

In the spring, once the temperature is above 41°F (5°C), the garlic greens start to show. Cut some of the stems and use them as chives. The garlic vegetative growth rests during the summer while the garlic body swells and in late summer it is time to harvest. Always use controlled seed onions from a plant nursery to avoid plant diseases.

Garlic—first-rate varieties

"Primor" produces early small, strongly lilac-colored bulbs with 6–14 cloves. Grows a flower stem and top bulb. Hardneck.

"Sprint" is an early, average-sized light lilac bulb with 7–12 even cloves. Grows a hard stalk (scape) with a flower and produces a top bulb. Hardneck.

"Messidrome" is an early, cold-hardy and reliable variety. White to rose colored and full flavor. It produces around 10–14 large cloves per bulb. Good for storing. Softneck.

"Germidour" is an early, big, violet garlic with a mild but full flavor. Produces 10–16 cloves per bulb. Good to bake or to grill. Softneck.

"Thermidrome" is somewhat early and has a mild and fine flavor. It produces big white bulbs with lilac streaks. Has about 10–16 cloves per bulb. Good to store. Softneck.

"Cledor" is a late variety with around 10–16 cloves per bulb. Good storage properties and good overwintering, Softneck.

"Printanor" is a late season, average-sized white globe garlic with 10–20 cloves. Softneck. Perfect for storing.

Cabbage

Kale and **Tuscan kale**, *Brassica oleracea,* are two easily grown and nutritionally rich leaf cabbage varieties which can be harvested repeatedly over a prolonged period. Kale has curly leaves, Tuscan kale leaves are more palm-like and chewy. These nutritionally loaded cabbage leaves have nearly reached celebrity status. Apart from this, they're tremendously worthy of growing due to their large crops compared to the small space their heads occupy.

Both kale and Tuscan kale can be directly sown as soon as the soil has reached 41°F (5°C), but it's beneficial to start them indoors as you will have plants ready to set out as soon as the season starts. Pre-cultivated plants are also sturdier and more resistant to possible attacks than those directly sown. Transplant into your garden when the risk for night frost is past. Give kale 1–2 ft. (40 cm–50 cm) and Tuscan kale 2 ft. (50 cm–60 cm) space between them. The larger spacing gives room for large lush plants while the smaller gives ample room to grow plenty of food. Harvest the leaves from the outside in, one by one, and the plant will still continue to grow.

Kale tastes best if it has been nipped by frost; and being cold hardy, it can be harvested in the garden bed throughout the winter. Tuscan kale can also take some frost, but is not quite as hardy as kale.

Kale cabbages—first-rate varieties

"Halvhög Krusig" is a classic (not heirloom) kale with broad, crinkly leaves. The plant grows 2–2½ ft. (50 cm–75 cm) tall. It isn't fully winter hardy but produces a large crop all the way to winter.

"Westland Winter" is a very hardy kale variety. Grows 2 ft. tall with solid plants and dark-green finely crinkled and very flavorful leaves. Can be left in the garden bed and the crop can be harvested throughout winter.

"Red Russian," or Siberian leafy rape, is a mild, tender, and very attractive kale. It's grayish green with violet stems and veins. It grows 1–2 ft. (40 cm–60 cm) tall. Not fully winter hardy.

"Baltisk röd" is a purple kale. The plant is dark violet all the way out into the leafy points. Grows 2 ft. (50 cm–60 cm) tall and produces a good crop. Turns dark green when cooked. Cold hardy.

"Black Magic" is a black (Tuscan) kale with long, narrow leaves and a palm-like growing habit. The plant grows 1–2 ft. (40 cm–60 cm) tall. Freeze hardy.

"Nero di Toscana" is a black (Tuscan) kale with dark blue-green leaves and light center vein. Grows 2½ ft. (75 cm) tall. Cold hardy.

Savoy cabbage, *Brassica oleracea* var. *sabauda*, is a beautiful cabbage, reminiscent of white cabbage, but has loosely bound heads and a more tender, mild flavor. Its advantage is that it's easier to harvest a successful crop, opposed to white cabbage. In addition, the cabbage moth seems to be less attracted to the wrinkled and crinkled leaves. Savoy cabbage demands less distance between plants than the larger cabbage varieties, which places Savoy cabbage high up on the No-Dig gardener's wish list. It is also great that it is cold hardy, and it can even overwinter under the snow.

A head cabbage's disadvantage is that it needs a long time to develop, and an early Savoy cabbage is ready about three months after being planted in the bed. You can pick off a leaf or two to eat while you wait for the head to form.

There are several varieties of Savoy cabbage, all with different shapes, color, harvest time, and hardiness. Early varieties can be directly sown in the soil once it has warmed to 41°F (5°C) although pre-cultivation is generally recommended to get strong and resistant plants. Later varieties definitely demand pre-cultivation to have time to get harvest ready. Set out the plants once the last frost date is past; it's enough to leave a space of 1 ft. (35 cm–40 cm) between the plants. Just like all cabbage plants, Savoy cabbage needs to change its growing bed each year and has to wait seven years to return to the former bed.

Savoy cabbages—first-rate varieties

"Vorbote" produces a dark green, slightly flattened head with a yellow interior. It is very fast growing and is also cold hardy. Easy to grow. Very suitable for early spring sowing as well as summer sowing for a late harvest.

"Vertus" is a French Savoy cabbage with deep blue-green puckered outer leaves, and with a sweet and mild heart. Reliable and easy to grow but not especially winter hardy.

"January King" gets beautifully purple crispy outer leaves in cold weather. It's frost hardy and can stay in the garden bed in the winter.

"Aubervilliers" is an early and tasty Savoy cabbage with beautifully savoyed leaves. It produces large oblate round heads. Tolerates only a light frost.

Leafy greens

Chard, Beta vulgaris, is of the Goosefoot family, which is closely related to the beet. Chard is easy to grow and very nutritious. Produces both early small leaves, and meaty, filling leaves once it's mature. Really a biennial, it's grown as an annual. Chard requires two months from sowing to harvest, and there are many red, yellow, and orange-stalked varieties. The green-leaved varieties produce the largest crops while the red-leaved tend to bolt. Chard continues to produce during the season; if the plants are trimmed to ¾ in.–1 in. (2 cm–3 cm) height while the leaves are still small they will return with renewed vigor. Sow chard when the soil has

Savoy cabbage "Aubervilliers"

Chard comes in many colors and
produces extended harvest.

warmed to 46.4°F (8°C), as the plant will bolt if the soil is colder. It's not necessary to start chard indoors but it's always nice to have plants on hand to fill in gaps in the planted beds. Chard also has a tendency to grow unevenly so it's good to have small plants at the ready. In some areas, chard can overwinter and will produce an early spring crop before it bolts. Cover the plants with straw and they will make it through the winter.

Chard—first-rate varieties

"Lucullus" has a medium thick, white stalk and yellow-green, dented leaves. Relatively frost hardy.

"Fordhook Giant" is sturdy and produces dark green leaves on thick, tender white stalks. It doesn't bolt easily, produces a large harvest, and can stand a few nights of fall frost.

"Erbette" is all green with large, smooth, spinach-tasting leaves on slim stalks. This one is harvested successively throughout the season and far into the fall. It can overwinter and produce an early spring crop.

"Magenta Sunset" produces medium-sized, slightly dented dark green leaves on purple stalks. Is both heat and frost hardy.

"Rainbow Chard" is a mix where the plants have stalks in white, yellow, orange, pink, and purple, while the leaves are green, purple, and bronze-colored. Gives a great touch of beauty to the garden bed.

"Orange Fantasia" has slim, orange-colored stalks with dark green, slightly dented leaves. Good to harvest early for small leaves.

"Golden Chard" has large, slightly dented green leaves on stark yellow stalks. Very nice flavor.

Lettuce, *Lactuca sativa*, exists in many different shapes but can be divided into three main groups: head lettuce, open-leaf lettuce, and cos lettuce. Open-leaf lettuce is the fastest growing; head lettuce forms loose heads; and cos lettuce produces tighter, upright growing heads. There are countless names, all with different colors and flavors. It's simple to find a favorite. Tests lots of different ones because lettuce is easy to grow and can be succession sown.

Lettuce grows best in cool weather with even moisture. The seed can be directly sown but it is also smart to pre-cultivate to have plants to set out as soon as there is an empty space in a garden bed. The seeds don't grow well in the summer heat. One trick is to fill the grow box with cold soil, broadcast seeds, and place the box in shade or in the refrigerator until the seeds have germinated. The emerging plants can cope with warmth.

Lettuce—first-rate varieties

"Black Seeded Simpson" is a nice, early open-leaf lettuce. The leaves are light green, crinkly, wavy, and juicy. The lettuce forms a loose head when mature. It copes with both drought and heat and is late to bolt.

"Cerbiatta" is an oak leaf lettuce that grows with upright, long lobed leaves. An open-leaf lettuce with strongly flavored outer leaves and mild yellow-green interior leaves. Fast growing, long-lived, and can cope with some frost.

"Merlot" is an open-leaf lettuce with shiny dark wine-red rumpled leaves with fringed edges. Creates a loosely closed head when mature. Lasts long before bolting.

"Red Cross" is a red-pigmented head lettuce where the meaty juicy leaves bind up into large beautiful heads. Can be succession sown throughout the season, and is both heat and cold hardy, and doesn't bolt easily.

"Speckled Bibb" is a head lettuce with apple green leaves that develop chestnut brown spots. Mild and delicate with fine flavor. The head is loosely bound with a creamy yellow interior.

"Little Gem" has an extraordinarily fine flavor. Produces small, ½ ft. (15 cm) tall heads. They are quickly ready for harvest and can be planted closer together than other varieties. They keep well in the garden bed.

"Jericho" is a cos lettuce with large compact heads and dented leaves. The head can grow to 1 ft. (40 cm) tall. Crisp with a sweet flavor. Heat hardy, but bolts easily after early sowing.

Spinach, *Spinacia oleracea,* is good and filling, provides loads of nutrition, and can be succession sown, except during the middle of the summer when it will bolt. There are many different varieties of spinach. Some have small leaves, others big, while others don't bolt so easily in drought conditions.

With a short growing period—approximately 40 days from sowing to harvest—there is no need for pre-cultivation. That said, it's always good to have plants growing and ready to fill gaps in the

SPINACH VARIETIES

New Zealand spinach, *Tetragonia expansa,* belongs to the iceplant (Aizoaceae) family, but tastes and is grown like spinach. It has a meaty texture and branches and grows larger the more it's harvested. Cut or pinch just above a leaf couple.

Malabar spinach, *Basella alba,* also Ceylon spinach, does not belong to the spinach family but to the Basella family. Grows like a tropical vine (lianas) and has meaty leaves. Needs to be pre-cultivated.

Go for a selection of lettuce
leaves to have a variety on
your plate.

SOW SPINACH IN WINTER

Spinach can be sown in winter, even on frozen soil as long as you cover the seeds with some thawed soil. It's easiest to sow in a pallet collar or other kind of grow box, because you can regulate the temperature with a lid. How to:

Scrape off any snow on the ground. Pour on a ¾–1¼ in. (2 cm–3 cm) layer of compost or soil. Make rows and lay down spinach seeds 4 in. (10 cm) apart. Cover with soil and then with a layer of snow instead of watering. The sun will eventually melt the snow. Cover with a transparent lid, for example, an old window or a frame with an attached plastic sheet. The seeds will be fine even if the soil freezes. Once spring arrives, the seeds will germinate and you can count on an early harvest.

garden beds. Spinach is excellent as a quick crop between other slow-growing crops. Especially those that will need room to spread after the spinach is harvested. The speed of growth also makes it possible to sow spinach late in the season and still have a harvest before winter.

Spinach germinates in cold soil, from 37.4°F (3°C) and up, although it's fussy during the summer in areas where the days are so long that there's little darkness at night. For this reason, in such areas, it's better suited as a spring and fall crop. Thin out early small leaves by removing crowded plants. That way the other plants have room to spread. Harvest successively as spinach continues to produce as long as the plant is left in the soil. Cut or scissor off the plants about ¾–1¼ in. from the ground or carefully break off the leaves. Harvest the whole plant if it is getting ready to bolt.

Spinach—first-rate varieties

"Bloomsday long standing" produces large meaty leaves. Can be sown early in the spring for a quick harvest but produces more if it is sown July–August. Is hardy to below freezing temperatures.

"Butterfly" is an early variety with large leaves. It bolts easily and is best suited for spring sowing until May, or from end of July and onward. Can overwinter.

"Matador" produces strong plants with arrow-shaped, dented leaves that have a blunt end. Can be grown year round and is quite late to bolt. However, early spring or later in the summer sowings produce the best harvests. This one is also known under the names "Viking" and "Atlanta."

"Medania" is quite early, producing large harvests of extra large dark green leaves. Doesn't bolt easily, even in places where the days are very long in summer months. Resistant to leaf mold.

PERENNIALS—EASY CARE AND A LONG SEASON

I have chosen the perennials below because they can be grown in areas with shorter growing seasons and they produce a decent amount of food. Some need a protected, well-drained location.

Daylily, *Hemerocallis* spp., produces edible buds and flowers. When freshly picked, they are very nutritious. Harvest them June to August and use in salads, soups, and stews or dry for later use. Daylilies have a laxative effect and should be consumed in moderation.

Daylilies grow well in both sun and light shade. They grow in clumps with large groups of fleshy rhizomes underground. They can grow 3½ ft. (110 cm) tall and to about 1 ft. (40 cm) in diameter. Daylilies are best propagated through division. Daylilies add an aesthetic touch and provide nectar and pollen, even if not a large amount.

Plantain lily, *Hosta* spp., is a beloved ornamental plant. Many are very surprised to learn that both shoots and flowers are edible. Young shoots are used like asparagus, the leaves work well for dolmas, and the flowers can be cooked or eaten raw in salads. The first shoots arrive in spring followed by the leaves in early summer, and the flowers in mid-summer.

Hostas like partial to full shade. They spread out considerably in clumps, and grow from 8 in. (20 cm) to over 3¼ ft. (100 cm) tall. Simplest way to propagate hostas is by division. Hostas can be grown in a range of hardiness zones but need a protected and well-drained location.

Poor Man's Asparagus, *Chenopodium bonus-henricus,* also known as **Good-King-Henry**, is a very nutritious plant of the goosefoot family. The early leaves can be used as spinach while the shoots can be eaten like asparagus, and the inflorescence like broccoli. The seeds can be used like quinoa. Poor Man's asparagus is harvested from May to October. It contains saponins so it is important to heat treat the parts before they are eaten.

Jerusalem artichoke "Bianca"

The Poor Man's asparagus plants need sun to partial shade and consistent moisture. Grows in clumps up to 2¼ ft. (70 cm) wide and can reach 1½–3¼ ft. (50 cm–100 cm) tall. It self-seeds freely. It is easily propagated through division. The plant can be started from seed but they need a cold period to germinate dependably. This plant thrives in protected and well-drained locations.

Orpine/Sedum, *Hylotelephium telephium,* is a very ornamental, lush succulent plant with edible crisp shoots and leaves. It is harvested from early spring to late fall. Eat it in salads or as raw sides. Soak tart plant parts to remove the bitter elements. Orpine blooms late, in August–October, making it a good plant for pollinators.

Orpine likes sun to partial shade. It grows in clumps to about 1–2 ft. (40 cm–60 cm) tall and spreads out to about 1 ft. (40 cm). Easily propagated through cuttings. Hardy throughout Sweden.

Jerusalem Artichoke/Sunchoke, *Helianthus tuberosus,* is grown for its wonderful, edible roots that are used in soups, salad, or oven-roasted whole. The roots can be harvested in late fall or in early spring once the frost is out of the ground. Pollinators appreciate flowering varieties.

Jerusalem artichokes like sun to partial shade. While the roots grow below the soil surface, the plant can grow to approximately 10 ft. (300 cm) tall. Propagation is by tubers that spread very easily. If you don't lay down firm boundaries it has a tendency to take over the bed. Grow the Jerusalem artichoke on one continuous surface to facilitate harvests and to disturb the soil less.

Horseradish, *Armoracia rusticana*, is a fine culinary flavoring. Apart from the root, shoots and the peppery leaves can be used in salads. The root is harvested from early spring until the ground freezes. The shoots and leaves can be harvested in spring and early summer. The leaves should be small when harvested.

Horseradish prefers sun to partial shade. It makes a rosette and grows up to 3¼ ft. (100 cm) tall. This rascal likes to spread so it needs to be planted where it won't disturb other plants. Renew the plant at even intervals for best flavor. Propagate horseradish by cutting off a piece of the root and planting it 1–2 in. deep. At the end of the season, dig up a piece of the root and store it in a cool dark area for replanting in the spring. Horseradish can be grown throughout large parts of the country in a protected and well-drained location.

Welsh onions, *Allium x fistulosum,* is a fast-growing hardy onion species with hollow stems and ball-shaped edible flowers. The stems are used like leeks or chives and taste best early in the season. Try them cooked or stir-fried. The flowers can be eaten in salads, although they can be a bit on the dry side. Welsh onions are harvested in July–September, and even later sometimes. Welsh onions give an aesthetic touch to the garden bed and are an asset for pollinators.

Welsh onions prefer shade. They grow in clumps to around 2½ ft. (80 cm). Propagation is done through onions or seeds. The seeds need stratification (i.e. time in a cold environment) to be able to germinate. Welsh onions like a protected and well-drained spot.

Rhubarb, *Rheum rhabarbarum*, is a long-lived perennial that is grown for its stalks. They are used to make cordials, puddings, preserves, and baked goods. Rhubarb is harvested in May–July. There is a lower amount of oxalic acid in the thinner stalks. Oxalic acid has a negative effect on calcium uptake and the kidneys. The plant's large leafy volume is an asset in mulched bed gardening.

Rhubarb prefers partial shade and likes to have damp feet. An established rhubarb plant can spread about 10¾ sq. ft. (1 m2) and grow up to 5 ft. (150 cm) tall. Fertilize with livestock manure in the spring and top dress successive layers of grass clippings around the plant during the season. The plant will continue to produce if you remove flowering stalks at the soil level. This plant is hardy throughout Sweden. The most common rhubarb variety is "Victoria," sports green and red stalks, produces heavily, and has a medium level of oxalic acid. "Elmblitz" is fairly early, produces abundantly, and has less oxalic acid. The flavor is tame. A later

Rhubarb is an early perennial that also provides material for mulched bed gardening.

variety, "Marshall's Early Red," produces a smaller crop and contains a high level of oxalic acid, but it's regarded as the tastiest variety.

Climbing spinach/Caucasian spinach, *Hablitzia tamnoides*, belongs to the spinach family but is, unlike its relatives, a perennial. The plant grows by climbing and it produces large quantities of spinach-like leaves. Top shoots can be used in soups, stews, and vegetable stir-fries.

The shoots are harvested starting in May and the leaves can be harvested until September. The climbing spinach loses some of its vegetable freshness once it flowers in August. Climbing spinach grows well in light to partial shade. It climbs to approximately 9–10 ft. (300 cm) but only spreads about 1 ft. (30 cm). The seeds are difficult to germinate and take a long time to get going. Preferably, they should be sown in the fall and be only lightly covered with soil. They can also be directly sown in the garden beds very early in the spring. The plant starts out hesitantly the first year but takes off vigorously the following year. It can be propagated by dividing the root shoots. Climbing spinach needs a protected and well-drained spot.

Turkish Rocket, *Bunias orientalis*, is an easily harvested cabbage plant that produces substantial, meaty clumps; it is sometimes called a perennial arugula. The entirety of the plant, including leaves, buds, and flowers, are edible. The plant is harvested in spring and summer and can be eaten raw. The plant is on the invasive plant list in some countries, so keep an eye on it to prevent it from taking over. Turkish Rocket flowers June–July and provides plenty of nectar so is a good pollinator asset.

Turkish Rocket likes sun to partial shade. It grows to about 2–3 ft. (60 cm–100 cm) tall and about 3 ft. (90 cm) wide. Self-seeding freely but can also be propagated by seed or by root cuttings. It needs even watering or the flavor is bitter. Grows best in protected and well-drained spots.

Patience dock/Monk's rhubarb, *Rumex patientia*, is related to garden sorrels like *Rumex acetosa* and *Rumex rugosus,* but has only a slightly acid flavor. Leaves and stalks are edible and are harvested in early spring and early summer. Early spring leaves are eaten raw while later leaves are good in stir-fries and stews or to make dolmas. The stalks taste somewhat similar to celery. The plant becomes inconspicuous in drought conditions but returns with new leaves in the fall. This plant contains oxalic acid.

Patience dock grows in full sun to partial shade, and can reach 1½–5 ft. (50 cm–150 cm) in height. It produces 1 ft. (30 cm) wide tufts. It is propagated by seed or through division. Patience dock prefers a protected and well-drained spot.

Ostrich fern/Fiddleheads, *Matteuccia struthiopteris*, is a fern with both ornamental and culinary properties. Ostrich fern (fiddleheads) is a delicate spring vegetable that is harvested in May, when it is around 2–6 in. (5 cm–15 cm) tall and just before the leaves start to uncurl. The young shoots are boiled for 15 minutes and then used in soups or omelets.

Ostrich ferns grow well in partial to full shade. They grow in imposing tufts up to 6½ ft. (200 cm) tall. They are propagated through division. Hardy throughout the whole of Sweden.

Colewort, *Crambe cordofolia*, is related to the better-known Sea kale, but grows much bigger and is heartier. Colewort is harvested from early spring to late fall and offers shoots and leaves, as well as buds and seedpods for consumption. Shoots, young leaves, and flower buds are lightly cooked; the buds taste somewhat like broccoli. Young seedpods can be mixed in salads.

Colewort likes sun to partial shade and it grows in tufty spreads of about 3¼ ft. (100 cm) and grows more than 6½ ft. (200 cm) tall. Pests attracted to cabbage easily attack it but the flavor is still good even if the leaves might look dull. It is propagated through division or root cuttings. Colewort is grown throughout Sweden and benefits from a protected and well-drained spot.

POLLINATION
& FLOWERS

Lately, vegetable gardening has started to go hand-in-hand with flower gardening. It's connected, of course, to the acute pollination crisis. It also has to do with what we eat. Whether we grow our food ourselves or it's grown by the food industry, it is dependent on insect pollination. There is a crisis currently because the number of bumblebees, solitary bees (i.e. wild bees), and honeybees, together with other pollinators, is decreasing sharply around the world.

The situation is especially tough for the bumblebees and the solitary bees, but honeybees are also at risk. The biggest threats are lack of nourishment and habitation in our landscapes and in our towns' hardscape environments. According to The Bee Conservancy, between 1947 and 2017, the honeybee population in the United States declined by 60 percent.

Wild bees, as well as cultivated (i.e. honeybees), are important for all biological diversity. If they get enough food in the form of carbohydrates from plant nectar, and protein from pollen, they will have enough stamina to flit from plant to plant, pollinating them to increase fruit and seed setting. This accommodates other insects, and birds and mammals get fed as well, and ensures even humans can consume to satiety.

Many eyes have, thankfully, been opened to the fact that it's vital to sow and plant vegetative growth rich in nutritious pollen and nectar. Many growers have stopped using chemical products, as well, since those are harmful for the pollinators. We are rewarded with gardens that are buzzing with life.

POLLINATION IN A NUTSHELL

Pollination is all about bringing pollen from the plant's stamen to the pistil (i.e. from male to female plant sex organs). The pollen grains are the equivalent of the human male's sperm, while the pistil, with its ovary, is the equivalent of the human female's uterus. Some plants are self-pollinating and can do the fertilizing themselves. More common is cross-fertilization where pollen from one flower is brought to another flower of the same species. The pollen distribution may happen by wind or with animal help, and that's where flying insects are extremely efficient. When an insect dives down into a flower to grab a bite, and to get food to bring back to the larvae, pollen gets stuck on their bodies and hitchhike to the next flower that can be fertilized.

COLOR CODING FOR INSECTS

Bees like bumblebees, solitary bees (i.e. wild bees), and honeybees prefer yellow and blue flowers. Butterflies find it easier to find red and violet.

Flowers in No-Dig garden beds

It works extremely well to grow flowers in non-dug soils. The principle for vegetables applies for flowering annuals and smaller perennials alike. A weed-killing layer of cardboard in the bottom of the bed, then a layer of compost or various kinds of organic cover materials provide a good environment for sowing and planting. If you want to set out a bigger plant it might be necessary to dig a hole through the cardboard to plant and then add plenty of soil or compost around.

Flowering kitchen garden

A weighty argument in favor of adding flowers to the kitchen garden is that flowers attract pollinators. Summer flowers thrive in the same kind of nutritious soil as vegetables, so it's a good idea to plant them together. It's a plus that companion planting contributes to keeping the soil healthy.

The smart way to get a quick start, with an even and attractive result, is to start the summer flowers indoors. Pre-cultivated plants are also strong and stand up well to pests and diseases. Closely spaced plants leave no space for weeds and they also retain the moisture in the soil.

To get a good layout in the garden beds it is helpful to choose the flowers with an eye to how they grow. This uses the growing surface efficiently in relation to the vegetables. The garden beds also look beautiful. A few things to keep in mind:

Border plants fill in well and can provide a flower edging to the vegetable beds, or create lush clumps in gaps in the beds. Suggestions:

Petunia, Nasturtium, Sweet alyssum, Pot Marigold. **"Anchoring"**
plants will pull it all together and make the planting look cohesive.
Suggestions: Purpletop Vervain, Cosmos Sensation, Nicotiana,
False Queen Anne's Lace.

Climbing plants start out from a smaller space but fill in efficiently
height-wise. Suggestions: Morning Glory, Sweet Pea.

Tall plants tower a bit over the rest of them and pair well with
ground covering vegetables. Suggestions: Snapdragon, Spanish
Mallow/Mallow Wort.

Create a meadow

Making part of the garden a meadow instead of a lawn gives you
a flowering and varied wild environment that will attract butterflies
and bees during a large part of the year. As many meadow flowers
are becoming rare, or are even endangered, this is a great way to
save species. A meadow is a thing of beauty and demands very
little effort once it is established. The following plants are beneficial
for butterflies and bees.

Butterfly plants: Dianthus, Purple Loosestrife, Scabiosa,
Goldenrod, Primula, Yellow Bedstraw, Campion, Common
Milkwort, Everlasting, Marjoram, Red Campion, Radiant
Cornflower, Heliantheum, Rough Hawkbit, Catch-Fly, Knapweed,
Field Scabious, Cuckoo Flower, Dog Violets, Devil's Bit.

Bumblebee and Honey Bee plants: Columbine, Spiked
Speedwell, Pasque Flower, Creeping Thyme, Ornamental/
Melancholy Thistle, Purple Loosestrife, Scabiosa, Kidney Vetch,
Yellow Iris, Primula, Yellow Bedstraw, Bitter Vetch, Geum Rivale/
Water Avens, Marjoram, Bird's Foot, Bluebell, Sweet Violet, Ox-eye
Daisy, Red Campion, Radiant Cornflower, Wood Forget-me-not,
Peach-leaved Bell Flower, Sea Thrift, Field Scabious, Common St
John's Wort, and Devil's Bit.

FLOWERS FROM SPRING TO FALL

By planting a combination of flowers that bloom at different times during the seasons, insects are provided with consistent access to a variety of food. It is especially important to plant early flowering nectar and pollen providers, giving dazed and newly emerging insects nutrition early in the spring when there is little on offer in nature. Even plants that are not yet full of pollen and nectar are important because "something is better than nothing."

The plants below are all perennials unless otherwise noted. The flowering time is approximate and depends on where you're gardening and how the season develops.

Snowdrops and **Winter Aconite** bloom from February.

Cornelian Cherry can flower starting in February.

Pussy Willow and **Willow** flower early in the spring and are important nutritional sources for newly emerged queen bees which are going to feed the larvae and warm the nest. Choose male plants as they are beautiful and will provide plenty of pollen and nectar. The female plant is more insignificant and doesn't offer quite as much to eat. Or plant one of each.

Crocus flowers in March and has lots of pollen.

Hazel flowers in March–April.

Squill and **Pearl Hyacinth** flowers from April.

Raspberries can start flowering already in April and are rich in nectar.

Cherries flower in April–May, providing large amounts of both pollen and nectar. Choose a variety hardy in your gardening zone, and preferably hardier in one or two more if the trees will be planted in a cold and draughty spot.

Apples flower in the middle of May and offer a large amount of pollen and nectar.

Red/black/white currants flower in May.

Hagberry/Bird Cherry flowers in May and provides both pollen and nectar, in addition to attracting butterflies in droves.

Lilac flowers in May–June.

Dandelion flowers in May–June.

Borage flowers in June and is perfect as bees like the color blue. Borage also comes in white. This is an annual that is sown in a sunny spot in spring and willingly self-seeds later on.

White clover/Shamrock blooms with a waft of honey fragrance from early summer throughout the season and offers lots of nectar and pollen.

Lavender provides pollen and nectar and flowers the whole summer.

Herbs like **Marjoram** or **Oregano** attract insects during the whole summer and have a lot of nectar.

Orpine/Sedum flowers starting in July, provides a lot of nectar, and attracts butterflies with its violet color.

Phacelia flowers from July to September. One of the best flowers for attracting bees and butterflies. This one is also used as a green cover crop.

Hyssop flowers from July to September and gives a lot of pollen and some nectar, and attracts butterflies.

Purpletop Vervain flowers from July until frost and is a magnet for bees and butterflies. It provides lots of nourishment in late summer. It is a perennial in warmer areas but is otherwise grown as a summer flower.

Butterfly Bush/Buddleia flowers from July to September and its color attracts butterflies. *Buddleja Davidii* is the hardiest.

New York Aster flowers from August to October and is rich in pollen. New York Aster is really a selection of various perennial asters, collected under one name.

Common Ivy flowers in October.

GREAT BUTTERFLY BEDS

Butterflies can easily find red and violet colors. That's why a planting with red and violet plants will attract lots of pollinating butterflies to the garden. This combination of perennials delights both humans and butterflies, and even bees will be tempted to take a closer look:

Kamchatka Bugbane, Anise Hyssop, Masterwort, Mountain Fleece, Peach-leaved Bell Flower, Joe Pye Weed, Scabious, Purple Loosestrife, Bowman's Root, Purple Moor Grass, Wild Marjoram/Oregano.

Other ways to attract insects

- Water is vital to bees. A water reflection created by a pond or a bird bath will make the bees put their energy into pollinating instead of searching for water. Place a few pebbles in the water for the insects to sit on so they don't risk drowning.
- Bumblebees build nests in porous moss, in tufts of grass, or in natural dens like deserted mole dens, hollow trees, or empty spaces in walls. A bumblebee's dream home can be made from clay pots and roof tiles that are partially submerged in the ground. Create a small settlement from terracotta pots and old broken roof tiles.
- A wooden log with a number of 4–8 in. (10 cm to 20 cm) -long holes in one end makes a great bee hotel. The bees will lay eggs and store pollen in the spaces. Make the holes with alternatively a ³⁄₃₂ in. (3 mm) and a ½ in. (13 mm) drill. Place the bee hotel in a dry, sunny, and protected spot.
- A bunch of sawed off bamboo sticks tied together, dried Jerusalem artichoke stalks, or hollow elder or raspberry branches can become a smaller version of a bee hotel. The bees use the hollow spaces for laying eggs and storing pollen. Place the hotel in a dry, sunny, and protected spot.
- Build an overwintering nesting box for butterflies. It is the same idea as a birdhouse except that the front has several ³⁄₈ in. (10 mm) thin slits instead of a hole. Fill the nest with coarse bark and place it in a sunny, protected spot near flowers that butterflies enjoy.
- A clump of growing nettles in a corner of the garden is a perfect nursery for butterfly larvae.
- Prepare a sandy area—a bee bed—where the female bee can dig a nest to have and to feed the larvae. Prepare it in an open, well-drained, and sunny area, protected from the wind, and no farther than a few hundred yards (100 m) from flowers.

A log and a few bunches of reeds and bamboo sticks pushed in between a few planks on the wall = a perfect bee hotel.

THUGS IN THE GARDEN BED

The reason that a No-Dig garden is usually free from bigger problems is that an undisturbed and mulched or composted soil is healthy and flourishing and the soil organisms are allowed to do their work in peace and quiet. Of course, even a No-Dig garden can get into problems, but there's no need to reach for a spade or chemical treatments. You have to be knowledgeable, protect, prevent, and in some cases fight the baddies with biological or physical plant protection materials.

Prevention

Prevention is the key to avoiding diseases and pests. Check list:

Undisturbed soil. When the microorganisms in the soil are allowed to do their work, harmful fungi and diseases have difficulty getting a foothold.

Covered beds. Health-promoting microbes increase in the soil when the garden beds are covered with compost and/or organic mulch materials.

Crop rotation. Overwintering pests and diseases are prevented from doing considerable harm when you practice crop rotation.

Balance. In a flourishing garden, you don't just find vegetable beds but also flowers, bushes, trees, and nooks and crannies that attract butterflies, bumblebees, honeybees, and other insects. The insects contribute by pollinating and many also feast on pests that would otherwise destroy the plants.

Hygiene. Clean tools and pots don't spread disease and pests, and sharpened tools don't cause damage where disease can take hold. Healthy seeds and resistant plants are prerequisites for successful gardening.

DIY INSECTICIDAL SPRAYS—RECIPE AND USE

Insecticidal soap chokes lice, spider mites, and larvae. Mix ¼ cup (½ dl) pure liquid soap (no fragrances, moisturizers, etc.) in 4¼ cups (1 liter) water. If you want, add 1 tablespoon methylated spirit. Pour into a spray bottle. Pick off as many pests as possible, then spray the plant leaves, both on top and underneath so any pests left are fully covered. Repeat the treatment after four or five days. Repeat at least three times.

Garlic water works against powdery mildew and might even frighten off insects. In a large saucepan place three peeled and crushed garlic cloves in 8½ cups (2 liters) of water. Bring to a boil. Strain off the garlic. Mix in two teaspoons of pure liquid soap. Remove the affected plant leaves. Spray the rest of the leaves with garlic water. Repeat the treatment two to three times a week until the plants don't look mildewed any longer.

Baking soda solution works on mildew so the fungi cannot reproduce. Mix a tablespoon of baking soda with 4¼ cups (1 liter) of water and one tablespoon of canola oil. Spray the whole plant and don't forget the underside of the leaves. Repeat this two to three times a week until the plants no longer look mildewed.

Control. By keeping an eye on the growing plants you can make sure that diseases and pests don't have a chance to get established. Nip off affected leaves and plant parts, remove fruits affected by rot, and pull out sick-looking plants.

Pest Control

Biological pest control methods use organisms that are placed in the beds. The pests are fought by the introduction of their natural enemies. It can be green lacewings against aphids, Hypoaspis mites against fungus gnats, or nematodes against slugs. Biological treatments are gentle to plants and pollinators. The treatments are often bought online and usually contain living organisms that need to be used immediately upon delivery.

Physical pest control, also called insecticidal soap, fights the attacker in several ways. Soaps and oils can choke or make eggs or fungal hyphae wither. Other insecticidal soaps strengthen the plant's cell walls or stimulate the creation of defense substances that increase the resistance against, for example, fungal attacks.

Protective fiber cloths and netting

A row cover keeps the ground warm after early sowing, protects plants against frost, and stops insect attacks. Fabric stops these insects: carrot root fly, cabbage root fly, onion fly, carrot psyllid, flea beetles, and caterpillars. Place the fabric so it overlaps the bed slightly and anchor it well. The fabric can stay on until harvest. Get a sturdy fabric, ¾ oz., 10¾ sq. ft. (22–23 gr/m2), which will be slightly more expensive but will last longer than a cheaper fabric. Buy a roll and share with gardening friends.

Insect netting protects against cabbage root fly, carrot root fly, and various cabbage moths. It also

A row cover can stop insects from marauding, but it has to be placed correctly, and without any gaps.

gives some protection against flea beetles. Insect netting lets in light and water, gives good protection against wind, but doesn't raise the temperature or protect against frost. Place the netting over the bed and anchor it with clamps or clips and cover the edges with soil to seal it. Leave the netting in place until harvest. Insect netting is sold in rolls.

A windproof floating row cover, woven of small transparent ribbons that won't separate when handled, is another option. The net protects against bird attacks and bigger pests like moths /butterflies, but not against the smallest pests. It works best when placed over tunnels and is anchored with sand bags or planks. Leave it on until harvest time. It is often sold in large 6½ ft. or 13 ft. (2 m–4 m) -wide sheets.

COMMON PESTS AND HOW TO GET RID OF THEM

Aphids are ¹⁄₁₆–³⁄₃₂ in. (2 mm–3 mm) long and come in colors from black, red, and green, all the way to white. Aphids collect in large groups on the underside of leaves or on the top of shoots, where they suck the moisture from the plant destroying the stems and leaves. They also secrete "honeydew" which attracts soot mold fungus (not harmful to plants), which covers the leaves in a dark coating.
Treatment: Remove the aphids frequently by hand. Crush the egg collections. Spray with water. Spray the aphids with potash solution at least three (3) times with four (4), five (5) day intervals.

Mealy bugs/White flies are ³⁄₆₄–¹⁄₁₆ in. (1 mm–2 mm) long and look like small butterflies. White flies suck the moisture from plants, damaging them. The white flies also secrete "honeydew" which attracts sooty mold fungus (not harmful to plants on its own) and it covers the plant leaves with a dark coating.
Treatment: Pick off eggs and larvae manually. Spray with water. Spray the flies with insecticidal soap to choke them.

Flea beetles are ¹⁄₁₆–¹⁄₈ in. (2 mm–4 mm) long, black and yellow-striped or dark colored. They like dry and warm soil. Flea beetles do damage by, among other things, gnawing holes in cabbage plants and radishes. The flea beetles head initially to the newly emerging plants.
Treatment: Water the soil thoroughly—flea beetles do not like damp

soil. Cover with garden fiber fabric. If the flea beetles still turn up, spray them directly with a strong jet of water and they will leave. Start cabbage plants indoors. Strong and sturdy plants have more resistance against attacks. Also pre-cultivate Chinese cabbage and plant out as a lure together with other cabbage plants. Flea beetles tend to eat the Chinese cabbage first as it is easier to digest. That way the other plants have time to grow and become more resistant.

Wireworms are up to 1¼ in. (3 cm) long, hard-shelled yellow larvae that burrow tunnels in potatoes and carrots. They normally live off grass roots but can be left behind in the grassy area that is turned into a garden bed. The second year tends to be the worst as the grass roots are finished and the wireworms turn their attention to the vegetables.
Treatment: Don't grow potatoes or carrots the second year after you've turned a grassy area into a garden bed. Manually remove all visible larvae.

Cabbage moths are white with black points and spots on the wings. They lay small yellow eggs on the underside of cabbage leaves. The eggs develop into yellow-green, 1½ in. (4 cm) larvae with black dots. The larvae gobble up the cabbage leaves.
Treatment: Cover the cabbage crop with a cabbage net or floating row cover to stop the cabbage moth from entering. Check each day, especially under the leaves. Crush the eggs and manually pick off the larvae.

PESTS VERSUS BENEFICIAL INSECTS

Hoverflies, Common Green Lacewings, Earwigs, Ladybirds, and Wasps will dine on hundreds of pests a day. The Carabid beetle is a small insect that rushes around on the ground eating insects and larvae. The parasitic wasp—a wasp with thousands of species—lays its eggs in aphids, cabbage moth larvae, and beetle larvae. All of which will die when the parasitic wasp's larvae hatch and eat the host insects from the interior. We admit willingly that beneficial insects are just wonderful! This does pose a dilemma. At the same time as we mentally hug our insect friends, we don't want to welcome the pests. Although, the hard truth is, having beneficial insects means we must also have the pests. Both kinds are equally sensitive to preventive treatments. If you start spraying the pests with insecticidal soaps some of the beneficial insects will fall foul, too. The only solution left to prevent this from happening is to remove pests manually or try to rinse them off with water.

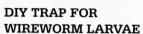

DIY TRAP FOR WIREWORM LARVAE

To get an idea of how many wireworm larvae you have in your soil, dig a hole approximately 6 in. (15 cm) deep and place half a potato in the hole. Cover with soil. After two (2) weeks remove the potato and take a look. Don't plant potatoes in that bed if you find wireworm larvae.

Carrot root fly, onion root fly, and **cabbage root fly** lay their eggs in the soil, alongside the plants. The eggs hatch into larvae that eat on the plant roots. The larvae can overwinter in the soil. The Carrot root fly is about 1/8 in. (3–4 mm) long, black with yellowish head, yellow legs, and transparent wings. The Onion root fly is light gray, between 3/16–5/16 in. (5 mm–8 mm) long, with black legs, and wings with yellow edges. The Cabbage root fly is around 3/16 in. (5 mm–6 mm) long and looks like a common housefly but is gray-brown with red eyes and a silver white head.

Treatment: Plant in raised beds because the flies don't fly higher up than around 1 1/4 feet. Practice crop rotation.

Ants steal newly sown seeds, build nests in the ground, and help aphids survive.

Treatment: Water thoroughly as ants prefer dry soil. Remove the ant nest and pour boiling water in the hole. A sprinkling of cinnamon on the soil can get the ants to disappear in a few days.

Nematodes, also sometimes called **hookworms**. These are usually beneficial, working the soil and destroying pests. They are often used as organic pest control. Some nematodes do attack vegetables, especially the ones within the nightshade family and appear mostly in depleted soil. The plants get dwarfed, branching root systems and poor vegetative growth. The worst of them is the potato cyst nematode, which can stay in the soil for up to twenty (20) years.

Treatment: Grow in mulched and composted garden beds. Plant Marigolds. The marigold secretes a substance the nematodes dislike. Practice crop rotation. The nematodes will starve to death when they don't have a host. Grow resistant plant varieties.

Chinch bug/Barber beetle or **Stinkbug**. There are hundreds of species of these pests, and many of them secrete a nasty-smelling substance. The bugs look like beetles but are not closely related. Their color is often a discreet green or brown and the overlapping wings lie

Cabbage caterpillar

Gray slug

Spanish slug

close against the body. Depending on variety they usually grow to
⅔–¾ in. (½ cm–2 cm) long. The bug attacks and sucks moisture from
tender shoots and leaves with its proboscis. Young shoots wither just
above the attacked area, and larger leaves are chewed up.
Treatment: Cover with garden fabric.

Slugs and **snails/molluscs** eat every crop they encounter in the
garden. Snails/molluscs have shells while slugs are bare. The
Spanish slug, better known as a "murder slug," is the worst. It is
3¼–6 in. (8 cm–15 cm) long and reddish or dark brown.
Treatment: Water in the morning instead of at night—snails/molluscs
and slugs are nocturnal and are encouraged by moisture. Pick off
slugs and snails/molluscs by hand and chop them in two just behind
the head or place them in boiling water. There are also several slug
baits you can buy.
- Iron phosphate. Pellets charged with iron phosphate and a
  substance that attracts slugs and snails/molluscs are placed on
  the ground. Once they have eaten the pellets they stop eating
  and starve to death. The pellets are sold in plant nurseries.

WATCH OUT FOR THE GRAY SLUG!

It's a myth that the **Gray slug,** *Limax maximus,* is beneficial and keeps the Spanish slug away. The gray slug eats mainly dead plant matter but will also consume growing perennials and small plants. It will devour certain dead insects and their eggs but it doesn't go for other live slugs and snails/molluscs. The gray slug is native to Europe but has spread to the United States. The gray slug can become a real problem in a changing ecological environment so we need to keep it from spreading.

DIY SNAIL/MOLLUSC TRAPS

Snails/molluscs like carrots. Lay down pieces of carrots and the snails/molluscs will arrive, leaving everything else alone. The carrots are also perfect traps because the snails/molluscs congregate, making it easy to catch and eliminate them.

- Nemaslug, a product made containing larvae of the nematode *Phasmarhabditis hermaphrodita,* a bacteria-eating hookworm. The product is mixed with water and then watered over the soil where the nematodes will search out slugs and snails/molluscs and infect them. The snails/molluscs and slugs die within 4–18 days. These nematodes kill snails/molluscs and slugs but are harmless for other insects. Nematodes are easily ordered online but, because they are a live organism, they need to be used within one week of arrival.

Start fighting snails/molluscs and slugs in the spring while their population is still limited and the young ones are not yet laying their eggs. Keep treating throughout the summer. Make a last raid in October, just before they go into hiding over winter, and you'll see less of them in the spring. Never put dead slugs and snails in the compost— instead, throw them in the garbage can.

Birds are mostly beneficial but they do have a penchant for newly sown seeds and can gobble up berries and fruit in a jiffy.
Treatment: Protect sown seeds and developing fruit with row cover. Avoid netting as birds can get tangled up and injured.

Deer, hares, and rabbits: they eat everything unless it has a very strong odor.
Treatment: Fence the garden bed area. You'll need fine-mesh netting against rabbits and hares and it needs to be anchored well against the soil. The net might even need to be dug down into the soil about 1 ft. (30 cm).

Voles and **moles** dig tunnels and munch on roots, bulbs, and onions down in the soil.

Treatment: Set out noisemakers and vibration devices that are sold in stores and online. Buried empty bottles with the neck sticking up can catch the wind and give off a whistling sound that is unpleasant to the pests. Place vole traps in active tunnels, setting the traps with pieces of carrot. Check the traps several times a day, and change tunnels as the vole learns very quickly what to avoid if there is something suspicious.

COMMON DISEASES AND HOW THEY APPEAR
Bacterial attack
If a plant is damaged, bacteria might enter and kill the plant. It is often the grower who spreads the bacteria through their hands or dirty garden tools. Some signs are similar to nutritional deficiencies, but over time you'll learn to spot the difference. Signs of bacterial attack on your plants might be:

- dry or brown spots on leaves
- withered parts on leaves
- withered and brown edges on leaves
- black veins in leaves
- limp and withered plant
- rotten stem
- tumors or growths on plant

Treatment: Bacterial attacks are not treated. Remove the dead plants.

Viruses
Viruses are microorganisms that can cause disease. There are hundreds of plant viruses that damage plants in myriads of ways. The most infectious are tomato and cucumber mosaic viruses, which cause deformed and mosaic-patterned leaves, weak root development, weak vegetative growth, and a rotten harvest. Viruses are most often spread through aphids, plant fluids, seeds, infected plants, and tools.

A NORWEGIAN METHOD TO FIGHT SPANISH SLUGS
For many years, to fight off Spanish slugs, the Norwegians have used the knowledge that Spanish slugs are cannibals and will eat their own. The method is to collect as many slugs as possible, kill them and infect them with Nemaslug, a nematode slug bait. This results in a continuous treatment cycle that kills the slugs. The method was pioneered by Norwegian agriculturist Torstein Mo.
How to:
• Collect as many slugs as possible. Cut them in half and place them in a bucket of Nemaslug diluted in warm water.
• Let the slugs soak in the solution for a few hours—it's best to have them prepared for the evening. Let the bucket stand in a cool spot, never in direct sunlight.
• Pour the snails into a strainer. Save the leftover solution. Spread the infected slugs evenly all over the garden, preferably in shady and humid areas that slugs prefer. Water with the leftover solution in slug-infested areas.
• As the slugs die off they become food for the new slugs that get infected by the nematodes and die, becoming food for new slugs that will also die, ad infinitum.

Powdery mildew lies like a white layer on the plant
and sucks all the nutrition from the plant.

Treatment: Practice good garden hygiene. Keep plants free of lice and other pests. Remove infected plants. Grow resistant plants.

Fungal diseases

These are found both above and below ground and can spread by the wind and through the ground. Fungi like a humid environment.

Sclerotinia stem rot/White mold is a fungal disease that attacks plants including: dill, beans, cucumbers, and lettuce. The stems become soft and wet, and then they rot. A white mycelium develops in the rot and the stems get fruits that develop new spores. This fungus can also attack stored root vegetables. This fungus is infectious and can survive in the soil for several years.
Treatment: Remove sick plants. Practice crop rotation.

Gray mold likes to attack weakened plants. It is often strawberries, cucurbits, bell peppers, and tomatoes that are attacked. The plants lose color, become brown and watery, and finally a moldy gray brown. Later fruit develop in stems and produce more spores. This fungus also attacks stored root vegetables and cabbages.
Treatment: Choose fungus-resistant plants. Pre-cultivate. Use wider spacing between plants because the fungus likes humidity. Remove attacked plant matter. Lay off nitrogen fertilizer. Practice crop rotation.

Powdery mildew looks like a white floury coating found on leaves, flower buds, and stems where it sucks the nutrition from the plant. It is especially hard on cucurbits and berry bushes.
Treatment: Prevent by watering thoroughly during early dry periods. Remove infected plant matter, treat the others with insecticidal soap, baking soda solution, or garlic water (p. 196). Lay off any nitrogen booster. Increase potassium-rich materials as it strengthens the immune system. Choose resistant varieties.

Late potato blight is a fungus that attacks potato and tomato plants causing them to brown and wither. The fungal mold spreads easily to the potatoes or tomatoes as a brown rot that makes the crops toxic. Brown rot in potatoes shows in brownish shadows below the peel and later as reddish parts in the bulb.

- Nettle tea can help boost the plant's resistance to fungal attacks. Place nettles in water and leave in the sun for no more than three days. The process releases health-promoting substances into the water. Spray the plant leaves with the nettle water. As they absorb the water the whole plant is strengthened.
- Horsetail tea contains high levels of silicon that inhibits fungal attacks on leaves. Boil a handful of horsetail in 8½ cups (2 liters) of water for at least 20 minutes. Strain off the plant matter and dilute the horsetail tea 1:9 with water. Spray the plants sensitive to fungal attack with this tea as prevention.

Treatment: Plant early or mid-early varieties. Plant potatoes as early as possible to have a crop ready before Late Blight hits. Pre-germinated and pre-cultivated potatoes get a head start and will be ready earlier. Don't grow potatoes in an overly shady or humid area, as blight likes moisture. Go easy on nitrogen fertilizer as it benefits the fungus. Quickly remove any affected growth.

Potato wart is a soil-borne fungal disease attacking potatoes. The fungus parasitizes the cells in growing potatoes and causes subterranean tumors that grow uncontrollably. Fungal spores can stay in the ground for up to thirty years.
Treatment: Practice crop rotation. Plant potato-wart-resistant plants.

Brown fruit rot attacks damaged fruit producing rotten spots and yellowish spot circles.
Treatment: Remove damaged fruit, including damaged fruits that have dried on the vines/branches, to prevent disease spread before winter sets in because the fungus can overwinter, infecting next year's crop.

Clumpfoot disease attacks cabbage plants by the soil and causes inferior vegetative growth. The roots starve, become dwarfed, and develop tumors that stop the intake of nutrients and water. Eventually the plant dies. Clumpfoot disease can stay in the soil as long as 15–20 years.
Treatment: Remove affected plants. Don't grow cabbage or any cruciferous plant in infected soil for the next ten years. Practice crop rotation.

Wilting disease is soil-borne and often attacks legumes. Wilting disease makes the leaves curl up and wither and eventually the whole plant droops and withers.
Treatment: Remove affected plants. Practice crop rotation.

The flea beetles have been at work here.

SOME COMMON QUESTIONS

It is really very simple to practice No-Dig gardening. Unsurprisingly, there's bound to be a lot of questions that pop up. Here are some of the most common, and their answers.

If I want to practice No-Dig Gardening do I have to shut down my existing garden bed and start out anew?

Not at all! You can change your method immediately. Start adding compost and/or mulch to your existing garden bed. You'll want to check on how the plants are doing, and boost with fertilizer as needed. It might take a few years before the bed becomes nutritionally independent.

Can you touch the soil at all in No-Dig Gardening?

You can, of course, work the soil: hoeing weeds, building sowing rows, digging holes needed for planting, etc. If you're planting large plants with big or deep root clumps, you'll have to dig. Truth be told, gardeners have dug the soil throughout the centuries, and with good results. Both soil structure and its microorganisms are good at recuperating. However, you shouldn't bother them more than absolutely necessary.

I'm going to place a piece of tarpaulin over a piece of ground to choke weeds. Anything special I have to remember?

It's good to spread some compost or mulching material on the ground before you place the tarpaulin, to give worms and other microorganisms something to work with as the weeds break down. Make sure that there are no gaps. Any light getting through will encourage weed growth.

Does No-Dig Gardening work for clay soil?
Yes. Clay soil is perfect for No-Dig Gardening, especially as this soil is so hard to dig. Clay soil is very nutritious. As long as the microorganisms get mulch material and/or compost on top they will transform the clay soil to good topsoil. However, count on it taking a few years to be completed.

Is it really true you don't have to aerate or lift the soil with a fork or spade before starting a No-Dig bed?
Put away that spade! With organic plant matter on the soil, the soil organisms increase their activity and work to produce good structure for growing things. You can aerate with a fork if the soil is very compacted, but even then, it isn't really necessary.

Do you place compost and/or mulching materials in any special order on the garden bed?
Place the least decomposed material at the bottom and build up with mulch materials or compost. The higher up the material, the more broken down it should be. With finely decomposed compost at the top, you can sow and plant directly in it.

Do I cover the garden beds for the winter?
Never leave the soil bare. Continue to cover it even during winter to give the microorganisms something to work with. This also prevents weeds from getting a foothold in spring. In addition, the compost and mulch both protect the garden bed against weather and wind.

Where do I find mulch?
First thing to remember is that nothing growing in the garden ever leaves the garden. This means you'll use all the organic plant matter already there. Even if you're a keen gardener, it's not often

the garden can provide everything needed. Do ask neighbors and friends for their grass cuttings and old plant matter. Cemeteries and sports facilities can also save the day, because they usually have both grass clippings and leaves. (Unless it is a soccer field covered in artificial turf, of course.)

How thick a layer of mulch do I use and when?
A 4–8 in. (10 cm–20 cm) layer of mulch is enough as it prevents water evaporation, and also keeps the weeds in check. The more material you add, the more nutrients and humus elements are added to the bed and the microorganisms. A thick layer also insulates during winter so worms and microbes can continue their work. You can add mulch continually during the year.

I don't have a lot of grass clippings. Can I still grow in mulched beds?
Even a thin layer of grass clippings can make a difference in how much moisture stays in the soil and it does add nutrients. It can actually be an advantage to have thin layers of mulch materials in slug-rich environments because it makes spotting the slugs easier. The problem with thin layers is that they have a tendency to dry out and lose nutrients, plus it's easier for weeds to take hold in the soil underneath. Make a smaller bed and concentrate all your efforts there as it is more efficient and less work with thick mulch layers.

Do you need extra mulch material for more demanding crops?
Turn things around and imagine that you're growing the soil, not the plants. Demanding crops need good soil and poor soils need extra mulch material. It is all about adding different kinds of nutritious cover materials to the soil.

I understand that mulch preserves moisture in the soil, but what about compost?
Compost is also mulch, albeit in a processed state. When compost is in place on a bed it preserves moisture just as well as non-decomposed materials.

Can I place livestock manure in the fall and leave it over winter, or will the nutrients leach out?

Fully processed livestock manure is stable and retains nutrition. You can cover your garden with it in the fall if you're expecting a cold winter with frost and hard freezes. If the winter is warm, work will still go on in the soil. However, if there are no plants to actively take up the nutrition, it's likely to wash away with the rainwater.

Fresh livestock manure is a bit trickier. Mixing in straw, leaves, or other carbon-rich material will bind nitrogen better. It's all about finding a balance.

Bokashi compost has to be dug down in the ground. Does this mean that I can't use Bokashi when I practice No-Dig Gardening?

Of course you can use Bokashi! The secret is to let the Bokashi transform into soil in a soil factory and then place it in the garden bed. You can also create a lasagna bed with the Bokashi directly on the ground; adding layers of soil, old leaves, and plant matter. Don't forget to place a compost grill on top to keep away nosy animals.

Can you really sow and plant in compost and livestock manure? It sounds crazy!

You can both sow and plant as long as the material is well processed and has a good and crumbly texture. Don't grow in incomplete livestock manure as it will inhibit germination and burn delicate plant roots and stems.

Is it true that you never have to fertilize a No-Dig garden bed?

Yes and no. The soil's natural nutritional cycle is established about three years after starting a No-Dig garden bed, but you have to continue to add mulch and/or compost. If you grow crops closely and intensively they might need the boost of a fast-acting fertilizer. Biochar is excellent; just make sure it is charged with nutrients. In short, a soil is never done. You have to feed it continually.

My garden has difficult runner-spread weeds. Is it really true that I don't have to dig the soil before making my garden beds?

Please don't dig. It only gives the weeds new vigor. What you can do is loosen the soil with a pitchfork so you can easily remove the weed, root and all. Cover the ground with several layers of cardboard as you make the beds. Really bad weeds might need to be covered with black plastic for several years to be starved out.

I have slugs in my garden. Does mulching still work?

It might be worth it to fight the slugs, thinking how efficient and simple mulching is, just for its advantages. What's more, mulching usually produces stable and sturdy plants resistant to slug attacks. The alternative is making compost beds that don't provide the slugs with any decomposed material to feast on. On the compost bed, there is nothing to hide under so slugs are fully visible as they slither around. Otherwise, the order of the day, every day, is slug hunting with scissors in hand and decimating with iron phosphate or nematodes.

Can I use beech and oak leaves as mulch materials?

Oak leaves and beech leaves take a long time to decompose into topsoil. Both also contain tannic acid that acidifies the soil. We know today that vegetables prefer a slightly acid soil, but oak and beech leaves may make it too acidic. Beech leaves might also have growth-inhibiting effects. One trick is to finely shred the leaves with the lawn mower and mix them with other mulch material, starting up the decomposing process and balancing the pH level. The leaves can also be composted quietly in their own separate compost bin for several years. It's a good idea to layer them with grass clippings.

How do I stop grass from invading the beds?

This is one of the few times you do need a spade. If you don't have wide, covered pathways around the beds, you'll risk the grass encroaching on the bed. Once or twice during the season cut vertically with the spade along the garden bed, or dig a v-shaped ditch around the bed to reduce the risk of a grass attack.

INDEX

SOURCES

Books

Bokashi för en bättre jord, Peter Streijffert, Blue Publishing 2019.

Charles Dowding's vegetable garden diary, Charles Dowding, Permanent Publications 2019.

Den arbetsfria trädgården, Ingrid Olausson, Ruth Stout, Rabén&Sjögren 1971.

Fleråriga grönsaker—Upptäck, odla, njut, Philipp Weiss, Annevi Sjöberg, Daniel Larsson, Hälsingbo skogsträdgård 2016.

Gödsel—om trädgårdens näringsliv, Tina Råman, Bonnier Fakta 2016. [*Good soil, manure, compost and nourishment for your garden,* Publ. Frances Lincoln, March 2, 2017]

Handbok för köksträdgården, Lena Israelsson, Bonnier Fakta 2018.

Jordad—Enklare liv i kollapsens skugga, David Jonstad, Ordfront förlag 2016.

Lätt att odla naturligt—hur du lyckas med ekologiska odlingar, Eva Pettersson, OM förlag 2020. [*Sustainable gardening made easy; from design to harvest: how to grow organic, sustainable food in cold climates,* Publ. Eva Pettersson, March 21, 2021]

Klimatsmart trädgård—plantera och odla för hållbarhet, Susanna Rosén, Norstedts 2020.

Min dröm om lustgården, Börje Remstam, BR Tryck AB Börje Remstam 2018.

No Dig organic home & garden, Charles Dowding, Stephanie Hafferty, Permanent Publications, 2019.

Odla i pallkragen, Eva Robild, Ica bokförlag, 2014.

Rätt ur jorden—handbok i självhushållning, Bella Linde, Lena Granefelt, Ordfront förlag 2017.

Runåbergs fröer—grönsaker, kryddor och blommor för nordiska trädgårdar, Johnny Andreasson, Natur & Kultur 2013.

Skogsträdgården—odla ätbart överallt, Philipp Weiss, Annevi Sjöberg, Hälsingbo skogsträdgård 2018.

Stefans lilla svarta—Bokashi, biokol och bakterier, Stefan Sundström, Leopard förlag 2019.

Trädgårdsboken om jord, Håkan Wallander, Elisabeth Svalin Gunnarsson, Anton Sundin, Charlotte Permell, Alf Nobel, Magnus Nobel, Bokförlaget Langenskiöld 2016.

Permakultur! Framtiden i din trädgård, Ylva Arvidsson, Johan Arvidsson, Siri Arvidsson, Borrabo förlag 2017.

Lasagna gardening, Patricia Lanza, Rodale 1998.

Articles

Effektiva mikroorganismer—räddningen för miljön och jordbruket?, Karin Jansson, offprint, the journal *Odlaren* nr 1/2008.

Lär känna jorden, Rune Bengtsson and Eva-Lou Gustafsson, offprint, the journal *Hemträdgården* 2004, updated 2018.

Essays and Major Papers

Grönsaksoldling utan grävning—bördigare jord och mer näringsrik mat, Avalana Levemark, Swedish Bachelor's Thesis, Bachelor of Science in Conservation with major in Garden and Landscape Crafts, 2016.

Gödsling med urin, Göran Svanfeldt. Fact sheet organic growing nr 27, Riksförbundet Svensk Trädgård, 2013.

Hur påverkas genom odlingsåtgärder kan påverka mikrolivet i jorden—en litteraturstudie, Maria Olsson, Swedish Bachelor's Thesis, Swedish University of Agricultural Sciences, Uppsala, SLU, Horticultural Management Programme—Gardening and Horticultural Production, 2018.

Kompost för biointensiv odling—En studie av tillgången på material för ett kompostkrävande odlingssystem, Ebba Wilhelmsson. Swedish Bachelor's Thesis, Swedish University of Agricultural Sciences, Uppsala, SLU, Horticultural Management Programme—Gardening and Horticultural Production, 2019.

Recommended Websites and Blogs

deepgreenpermaculture.com
charlesdowding.co.uk
daylily-potager.blogspot.com
soilfoodweb.com

THANK YOU!

Niklas Vestin and **Rölunda jord** for cow compost and good advice.

Rikard Andersson, The Swedish Board of Agriculture Plant Protection Centre in Alnarp, who straightened out the concepts of aminopyralid and clopyralid.

Håkan Wallander, Professor of soil biology and environmental sciences at the University of Lund, for his kindness in answering knotty questions about life in the soil.

Johan Nilsson, landscaper and editor of the journal *Biodynamisk Odling*, for sharing his knowledge of composting, doing fact checking, and using pointed arguments for No-Dig gardening.

Lotta Fabricius Kristiansen, from the network Pollinera Sverige, for fact checking texts about flowers and pollinating.

Malin Sairio, bokashi.se, for fact checking the part about bokashi composting.

Emma Jansson for argumentation for No-Dig gardening, manuscript reading and for letting us photograph in your garden in Åkersberga.

Mia Blanche Settergren for great tips, manuscript reading, and photogenic plantings on the Bjäre peninsula.

Annika Gustafsson in Merlänna, Strängnäs, for conversation about growing, manuscript reading, and compost discussions.

Kristina Engdal in Krylbo, Avesta, for interest, manuscript reading, and lots of mulching tips.

Mats Christrup in Floby, Falköping, for good advice and manuscript reading.

Johnny Andersson and **Ina M Andersson**, Osprey Sweden Farm & Studio at Fogdö in Strängnäs, for exchange of experience and for being allowed to photograph your cultivations.

Elin Aronsen Beis, for talks about No-Dig soils and for permission to take the cover photo and photograph lots at the cultivations at Hufvudsta Gård in Solna.

Jessica Lyon, at OdlingsTV, who opened the cultivations at Tyresta National Park for our photography sessions.

Börje Remstam, mulch/compost gardener who generously shared his knowledge and also invited us to photograph his gardens outside Eskilstuna.

Cormac Donelly for allowing us to photograph in your garden over and over again.

The cultivation cooperative, **Under Tallarna**, in Järna, because you're inspiring and because we were allowed to photograph your biochar and lush soils.

Anette Nilsson in Boäng in Röstånga, for good advice about tall, weaver, and other plants that attract pollinators.

Helena Lindblom, quick and assured editor who encourages and questions with warmth and valuable insight.

Mikaela Haglund, Queen of proofreading, who has cajoled the smallest comma and full stop.

Pär Wickholm, true design professional with a feeling for a mad amount of fact sidebars.

Micke, Clara, and **Sofia Kristensen**, because you suffered kindly throughout all the different garden bed tryouts and photography sessions at home.

Malte Linde and **Dante Jernudd** for encouragement, ground service, and strict instructions to go down to the lake for a swim.

Frida Sandgren for always having a happy disposition and your earnest growing of our shared garden.